WALKING ON HIGH PLACES

KEYS TO KINGDOM LIVING

Leanne —

Sisters in Christ

Sandra Major

&

Louise Padia

SANDRA MAJOR & LOUISE PADIA

WALKING ON HIGH PLACES

KEYS TO KINGDOM LIVING

Pleasant Word
A Division of WINEPRESS PUBLISHING

ISBN 1-4141-0569-X
Library of Congress Catalog Card Number: 2005908608

DEDICATION

We dedicate this book to
all our faithful friends and partners
who believed in us and our ministry
from the beginning. We love and appreciate you.

CONTENTS

PREFACE

What is your life like? Are you walking in victory? Are you in the right job? Are you healthy? Is your family in good shape? Do you sleep peacefully? Do you have the kind of relationships that you desire? If you answered "no" to any of these questions, you will be glad you are reading this book! We do not have all the answers, but God does. What we have is experience in receiving God's promises and applying them to our lives. Our goal is to share this information, so you also can walk on the high places that David spoke of in 2 Samuel 22:34.

For us, it all began in 1982 when we submitted our lives to Jesus Christ. We did not realize at the time that we were in for the greatest adventure of our lives. Inviting Jesus into your heart and going to church every Sunday does not automatically mean you will walk in victory. In the beginning, we did not have the power in our lives that we have now, and it took us some time to receive the revelations of how to walk in victory. We could see victory in the Word of God as well as in people around us, yet while we knew it was available to us, it took time to learn how to have the victory in every area of our lives.

This is not the first book we have written. It is, however, the first book God has allowed us to publish. Twenty-three years ago, before we were saved, we had a very different manuscript on its way to the publisher. We were very deep into the occult, traveling the country and sharing our New Age beliefs. We had written what we thought was a wonderful self-help book to assist people in finding themselves and becoming better by becoming enlightened. What we did not know at the time was that the only true help comes from above, and the only way to become a better person is to be washed in the blood of Jesus Christ.

Thankfully, God stepped in and intervened on our behalf before the book could actually be published. Louise got saved in a beautiful, divine appointment, with Sandra's salvation not far behind. When we began our new lives, we left the old ones behind, including the speaking and writing "ministry" we were involved in, because we knew we were leading people astray and costing them eternal life. It was difficult, because we loved what we did. It seemed tailor-made for us, but we have come to realize that God created us for a purpose before we were born, and we were using the gifts He gave us to benefit the enemy. God is so awesome and so faithful and now, all these years later, He has brought us full circle. Since our conversion twenty-three years ago, God has been preparing us to fulfill His calling, and along the way He has taught us how to walk in victory every day. The book you have in your hands is the book He purposed for us to write to spread the word that we *all* can walk in victory. And when we do, we walk on high places.

ACKNOWLEDGEMENTS

Our special thanks to Heidi Geis whose friend-ship and editing skills were invaluable. God gave us the vision and Heidi helped us put it all to-gether. We also want to thank Jimmye Rose for her faithfulness and support in many wonderful ways.

FIRST THINGS FIRST

Matthew 16:13-15 (NKJ) says, "When Jesus came into the region of Caesarea Philippi, He asked His disciples saying, 'Who do men say that I, the Son of Man, am?' So they said, 'Some say John the Baptist, some Elijah, and others Jeremiah or one of the prophets.' He said to them, 'But who do *you* say that I am?'"

Jesus was telling his disciples that it did not matter who others said He was, only who they, as individuals, believed Him to be. This same question applies to us today. It only matters who *you* say He is, who He is to you—not to your best friend, not to your neighbor, and not to your spouse.

As we read on to verse 16, Simon Peter answers Him and says, "You are the Christ, the Son of the Living God." Christ was not Jesus' last name; it was a title given Him by his followers. The word *Christ* means "anointed of God," and by calling Him this name, they were admitting that He was God's Anointed One. This is where the name *Christian* comes from. It means "little anointed ones." In the days following the resurrection and ascension of Jesus, the Romans used the term *Christian* to label his followers in a negative way. They did not realize what a tremendous compliment it was. It is the same today. We, as Christians, carry the anointing in us.

Many people call themselves Christians. They think that because they were born in America and attend church now and then, they are Christians. They have no idea what the word actually means. If we are to be honest, we must ask ourselves if we truly are "little anointed ones." The only way the answer can be yes is if we have a living, personal relationship with Jesus Christ. Furthermore, the rest of this book will be meaningless to anyone who has yet to make Jesus Christ their personal Savior.

Romans 10:13 tells us, "whosoever shall call upon the name of the Lord shall be saved." Verse 10 states, "...with the heart man believeth unto righteousness; and with the mouth confession is made unto salvation." It is as simple as believing and receiving. If you have never taken this step, we want to encourage you right now to stop and sincerely pray. The exact words are not important, but we suggest that your prayer go something like this:

Dear Lord Jesus, I believe You are God, and that You died for my sin and rose from the dead. I admit that I have sinned and I ask You now to forgive me and come into my heart. Thank You for Your gift of eternal life. I accept it, and I want to live the rest of my life in victory, bringing glory to You.

If you have prayed this prayer, whether for the first time, or as a rededication, then we rejoice with heaven that you have joined the family of God and become one of His "little anointed ones." It is this wonderful, powerful anointing that is key to living a victorious life. God's Word is full of His promises regarding our future in Him.

We want to encourage you to put these promises to the test. A good example from our lives was when Louise began to attend bible school. She was a brand new Christian just learning how to believe God. Because she had never really studied the Bible before, she did not even know the difference between the Gospel of John and First, Second or Third John. In fact, she was not really even sure who this John *was*. She felt totally inadequate and frustrated by the fact that her classmates all seemed to know so much more than she did about the Bible. So as she stood in the bookstore, looking at the three Strong's Concordances on the bookshelf, she knew she needed to have one in order to keep up in school, but at the time, she did not have the money to purchase one. She had heard sermons on God's faithfulness to provide for His children, so one morning she decided to find out if what she had heard about God was really true. Having heard a lecture the day before on believing God, her faith was strong. "Lord, I have got to have this book and you are the only one I can turn to," Louise prayed. She did not tell anyone else about it; only God knew about her need.

Two days later, only one concordance remained on the shelf. Louise's teacher, who almost always spent his break time outside walking and talking with God, came in from his usual walk that day and went to the bookshelf, picked up that last concordance, put it down on Louise's desk and said, "The Spirit of God told me to give you this." Louise became so overwhelmed that she fell on her face crying because she had just met the living Christ. It was a life-changing experience and from that moment on, Louise knew that God hears her prayers every time she talks to Him, and that He indeed is faithful to meet her every need.

CHAPTER TWO

AUTHORITY,
IT'S A LEGAL THING

Over the years, we have talked and prayed with thousands of people. Sadly, we find that the majority of them—and the church as a whole for that matter—are not living victorious lives. We believe the problem is that many Christians just do not understand their authority over Satan and the circumstances they face each day. By the time you finish reading this chapter, you will have a new perspective on the power you have over everything and a better understanding of what God has already done on your behalf.

Genesis 2:7 says, "...and the Lord God formed man of the dust of the ground and breathed into his nostrils the breath of life; and man became a living being." Adam came into being when God formed his body, but he became man when God breathed His very own breath of life into him.

Man is a spirit that lives in a body. Because he was made from the earth, God gave him authority over the earth. Because he was also made in the image of God, who is a spirit, Adam had authority *under God* in heaven. In creating Adam, it was always God's purpose and plan for man to have authority and dominion over both the natural and spiritual worlds. He told man to, "be fruitful and multiply, replenish the earth and subdue it and have dominion over the fish of the sea, the foul of the air and every living thing that moves upon the earth" (Genesis 1:28).

Once Adam had a living soul, God gave Adam *all* authority on the earth—including over the serpent, which came offering knowledge and equality with God. Adam knew he had dominion over everything in the garden including the serpent, but in that moment he lost sight of his authority. When Adam gave in to temptation and ate from the Tree of Knowledge of Good and Evil, he allowed Satan to strip man of his authority on earth, and in order for it to be reclaimed, God would have to become a man.

God had to become flesh to be legal here on earth. Any interference or influence in the supernatural on earth is only legal through mankind, so God, Himself, had to become flesh and dwell among us. He is a Spirit; therefore, He needed a body. It was the only way He could have the authority *on earth* to redeem man. God became man in the form of Jesus. He had to be born of a woman in order to buy back the dominion and authority that was given to Adam in the first place. After thirty-three years of walking this earth in the body of a man, Jesus gave his life on a cross and paid the high price of our redemption with his own blood.

Now we have the power and authority in the name of Jesus and His precious blood. That is why, when we make Jesus our Lord and Savior, the Spirit of God comes to dwell in us. Romans 8:11 tells us, "the same Spirit, that raised Christ from the dead, dwells in us." There is power and authority in the Spirit of God. What an awesome thought to ponder. His Spirit dwells in us, and as a result, we can do all things through Christ who strengthens us (Philippians 4:13).

The eighth and ninth Psalms tell us that all things were put under Jesus' feet. God has given Him a name which is above every name, and at that name, every knee shall bow and every tongue confess that Jesus Christ is Lord to the glory of God, the Father. When we use His name, we can cause healings to come, finances to increase, circumstances to change.

In Matthew 28:18, Jesus says, "All authority has been given unto me both in heaven and in earth. Therefore, *you* go into all the earth." In other words, you go preach the gospel everywhere. You take His name and you cast out demons and you lay hands on the sick and they will recover. He is talking to you! The authority is in His name, but Jesus commanded us to use His name and do these things. He wants us to realize and exercise the authority we have in His name. You see, until we understand our authority we will always end up being victims. God created us to be like Him. As Christians, it is our responsibility to overcome in every situation, good or bad, and to walk in victory all the days of our lives.

Our point here is that God has already done His part. He has already equipped you. He has already given you everything you need. What you need to do is realize that instead of heading to the victory, you already have the victory. Do not beg and plead and ask God to do things. Instead of begging God, we need only stand and believe His promises.

We cannot talk about power and authority without talking about the laws that govern them. Laws are simply rules and regulations. Authority comes from rules that are non-negotiable. There are spiritual laws and physical laws. Some people believe the commands of God are just concepts or suggestions. They believe in a relative morality that changes with the social climate. This is not the case; we are subject to the immutable, inalterable Word of God. It is black and white; there is no gray with God. God's law is truth and it works when it is put to work to accomplish what God ordained.

Some people believe it is impossible to put God in a box; that we can never be sure what God is going to do. While we certainly cannot put God into a denominational box (because He may move in a new way, and we are not in a position to tell God what to do), one thing we know for sure is that God will never violate His Word. His Word is law. It is forever settled. In Psalm 89:34 God tells us, "My covenant

I will not break, nor alter the word that has gone out of my lips." When the Lord says something, it is binding. It is a covenant. We can count on it.

Psalm 138:2 tells us God has magnified His Word above His name. This is a bold statement, since the Jews considered the name of God to be so holy they would not even speak or write it. God is telling His people that while His name is holy, His Word is even holier. The first chapter of John very clearly spells it out for us: "And the Word was made flesh, and dwelt among us, (and we beheld his glory, the glory as of the only begotten of the Father) full of grace and truth." Jesus is the Word of God.

The Bible also tells us the name of Jesus is our strong tower; it is so powerful that every knee has to bow. The Word of God is exalted *above* even God's law. What a powerful statement! Yet in spite of this, people argue, "I know the Bible says '…by His stripes you are healed,' but you cannot put God in a box. You cannot say it is God's will to heal every time." They forget that God said, "I wish above all things that you should prosper and be in health, even as your soul prospers" (3 John 1:2). God desires that we be healthy and prosperous. The word *prosper* here means abundance, and God wants above all things that we have it in *every* area of our lives. When He says "even as your soul prospers," He is saying that the more you depend on Him and seek His face, the more you will see Him at work in your health and welfare. The better you *know* Him, the better you will *recognize* Him at work in your life.

Training ourselves to win is a process. If we are growing in Christ, we should be experiencing more wins this year than last year. If things are not going well, we cannot blame God. We need to check and see if we have been exercising our authority. Do we *really* believe his promises? If we answer no, then we need to pray and ask Jesus to help us conquer our unbelief. God says, "Faith comes by hearing the Word" (Romans 10:17). In today's world, there are so many ways to hear the Word of God. You can listen to tapes in your car, watch Christian television or listen to Christian radio. Saturate yourself in the Word, and do not stop until you believe.

FLIPPING THE SWITCH

Hebrews 1:3 says Jesus is "...the express image of His person and the brightness of His glory and He upholds all things by the Word of His power." This passage refers to all of creation. The Word of God holds creation together because, as Genesis tells us, God spoke everything into existence. He ordered the world to do things. It functions and is based on the commands or the words of God. The logical conclusion here is that if God were to break His Word—just one promise—the universe would cease to exist because it is held together by His Word. If God's Word is ever compromised, His creation is compromised and would self-destruct. God cannot break His Word, and yet there are people who say, "I know what God said, but He is sovereign and can do whatever He wants to." Yes, God can do anything—anything but violate His Word.

As Christians, we need to take some responsibility for what does and does not happen in our lives. Because God has given us freedom in our lives, it is possible for us to limit Him from accomplishing His will on our behalf. Our every choice, good or bad, carries consequences, good or bad. Psalm 78 tells us about the children of Israel and their unbelief as well as the trouble they had as a result. Verse 37 says, "For their hearts were not steadfast with Him, nor were they faithful to His covenant. But He, being full of compassion, forgave their iniquity and did not destroy them. Yes, many a time He turned His anger away and did not stir up all His wrath, for He remembered that they were but flesh, a breath that passes away and does not come again." What a beautiful description of God's mercy for His children. He was not giving them what they deserved. His desire was to do them good. This idea is repeated for our benefit in Jeremiah 29:11, which says, "'for I know the thoughts that I think towards you,' says the Lord. 'Thoughts of peace and not of evil. To give you a future and a hope.'" The word *peace* here is translated from the Hebrew word *shalom*, which means nothing missing, nothing broken. That word, *shalom*, is what abundant life is all about.

God has a good plan for every one of us. He had an awesome plan for the Israelites. He was planning to bless them and be merciful to them, but they *would not let Him*. Verse 40 of Psalm 78 says, "How often they provoked Him in the wilderness and grieved Him in the desert. Yes, again and again, they tempted God and limited the Holy One of Israel." What an awesome statement. God's Word tells us right there that we *can* limit God and what He plans to do in our lives. People mistakenly assume that we cannot put any limits on God, but this scripture tell us differently; it says we can.

According to these scriptures, we *can* stop what God wants to do for us because God *gave us control over our lives*. God told us to choose, but if we are making the wrong choices we have the power to prevent God from operating in our lives. According to Romans 8:11, the same power that raised Christ from the dead already dwells in us. That is mighty power! The same power that it took to resurrect Jesus after three days in the grave is already at our disposal! What more do we need?

The key to this power is in understanding spiritual law. Spiritual law is no different than gravity or electricity. When the lights go out, there are specific reasons why. Most of us will not just sit in the dark and wonder why it is dark. We flip the light switch, or check the breakers. We may even need to go to the source—the power company. Once we have checked everything, chances are we will discover the problem, find a solution, and get our lights back on. Spiritual things like healing, deliverance and prosperity work in a similar fashion through faith, prayer and authority. God has established these for our own good. It is not His desire that we sit in our desperation and never wonder why everything is going wrong. It is our responsibility to search out the problems as well as the solutions.

Furthermore, these laws apply to all, even the unbeliever. Matthew 5:45 tells us that God makes the sun rise on the evil as well as the good, and He sends the rain to fall on the just and the unjust. He did this so we would not have to wonder if we could have access to it. Can you imagine if electricity only worked based on your character? You could only have access to it if you were a good person; if you were kind and you had not made any mistakes today, *then* electricity would work for you. How would you know if you could walk over and turn on the lights? Our God is orderly and systematic and He does not want us to wonder. He has already taken care of every detail; all we have to do is learn the law and put it to use. This is accomplished by reading the Word, by believing His Word and by acting on His Word through faith. Just as electricity is available to all, it is still up to the individual to flip the switch and make use of it.

CHAPTER FOUR

WHO THE DEVIL IS NOT

A common misconception among Christians is that Satan is omnipresent (all places at all times) and that he is omnipotent (all-powerful, invincible, unstoppable and supreme). These attributes are reserved for God Almighty only. Satan cannot be everywhere at once, or read our minds, but he has studied human nature for centuries and knows exactly how we operate. When we murmur and complain, he marks our weaknesses, and then uses them against us by simply depositing ideas and thoughts into our minds. Deception and suggestion are his greatest weapons and he always chooses his timing very carefully. By focusing on a particular need or desire he will attempt to lure us into a debate in order to cause us to begin to doubt God's word. His next step is to "help" us justify our wrongdoing, drifting away from God's Word and other spiritual things, such as tithing and praying. It is his desire that we take matters into our own hands instead of trusting God to provide the answer.

We need to remember that Satan is a liar and an outlaw, and Jesus has taken away his authority on this earth. Satan has no legal right to kill, steal or destroy the children of God, but he will try to do it anyway. He can only succeed if we let him get away with it, but it is our job to stop him. The Bible tells us we should resist the devil with all our might. He will put up a fight for a while, but if we persist, he has no choice but to flee from us. As long as we remain focused on God's promises, Satan has no power over us.

This is no easy task. We are bombarded by suggestions from the enemy every day in the music we listen to; the movies, news, and television shows we watch; the books and magazines we read; and even the people with whom we come into contact. We must resist by protecting our minds as God has instructed us.

The good news is that we can start this very moment to change our thinking by obeying God's Word. Romans 12:2 says we are to renew our minds daily. When we stop thinking a certain way, we will stop acting a certain way. Where our mind goes, our desires and behavior will follow. Golfers in the Pacific Northwest are perfect examples of this. During the winter when there is snow on the ground, they are content to stay inside and watch golf on TV or read about golf in the newspaper. At the first sign of spring, however, suddenly they are consumed with actually getting out and playing golf. It is all they think about. As soon as the courses are open, even if it is still cold and rainy, they are out there. Their minds have gone to playing golf, and it is only a matter of time before their desire and behavior push their bodies to follow.

We give the enemy too much power in our lives and too much glory for the things he does. Oftentimes, we blame Satan for things that happen to us as a result of our own doing. For instance, we blame him for attacking our bodies when our own poor nutrition or lack of rest is responsible. There are also spiritual laws in place that cannot be violated. For instance, the law of sowing and reaping: if you sow a bad seed, you will reap the consequences and then blame the enemy. The only power that our adversary has over us is the power we give him. Too many people are looking for devils behind every bush in order to avoid taking responsibility for their own fleshly, sinful decisions.

When Satan was kicked out of heaven because of his pride, he took a third of the angels with him. These demons are the ones assigned to torment and harass us. Paul explains in Colossians 2:15 that Jesus divested principalities and powers of their authority over redeemed people who live under Christ's lordship. The fact that Jesus made a public spectacle of them affirms that they are not eliminated—rather, their authority has been curbed. In 1 Corinthians

2:8, Paul goes on to say that Satan and his demons were completely confounded by the cross. They thought they had the victory. What a perfect example of Satan's limited ability to anticipate the ways of God. Because of the cross, we can be assured of ultimate victory through Christ. Isaiah 14:16 says we will gaze at Satan and say, "Is this the one who made the earth tremble?" The Bible also tells us in 1 Peter 5:8 that "…our adversary, the devil, walks about *like* a roaring lion, seeking whom he may devour." He is *not* a roaring lion, and the next verse tells us to resist him. Resisting him simply means to focus on God's words and not the lies of the harassing spirits. It takes diligence to ward off evil thoughts and we must be continually on guard against giving him place in our lives.

While Louise was attending a church in California, she was invited to be a member of a worship-dance team. This was exciting for her because she loves to worship God and this was a new and different way of doing so. A young girl who attended Louise's church was very upset when she was not invited to be on this team and, unfortunately, took her anger out on Louise one night after mid-week service. As Louise stood to leave her seat, the girl approached and bitterly lashed out. She verbally assailed Louise with hurtful and false accusations until Louise was in tears. This did not stop the girl's tirade, and slowly the tears gave way to anger. Louise stood tall, crossed her arms defensively and mentally prepared to do battle.

Meanwhile, Louise's husband Pete stood at the back of the church watching the scene unfold. At first he thought he might need to rescue Louise, but then he saw her demeanor change. Having been on the receiving end of one of Louise's lectures, he thought to himself, "Boy, this girl is going to get it now!"

Just as Louise was getting ready to put the girl in her place, the Holy Spirit spoke to her heart. "Stop. Drop your arms and stay in love." That was definitely *not* what Louise wanted to do, but with a bit more prodding, she obeyed. The girl saw her soften her stance, took it as a sign of weakness, and continued her assault.

Pete could watch no more. He came from his spot at the back of the church, took Louise by the arm and guided her up the aisle and out of the church. The girl followed them out, chirping all the way and only stopped once Louise and Pete were in their car with the doors shut. They drove away, hoping they would not run into the girl again. God had other plans.

The following Sunday morning, Louise took her place as a greeter at the church door. It was her custom to hug everyone as they arrived, but this presented quite a dilemma when she saw the girl coming through the door. Louise knew she had a choice to make. Her heart knew what God wanted her to do, but her flesh had other plans. The enemy whispered in her ear, encouraging her to avoid or ignore the girl, to snub her and teach her a lesson.

But in the end, Louise chose God and greeted the girl with a smile and a hug.

Louise made the difficult choice to do something she truly did not want to do, and God honored her. She behaved the way God wanted her to even when the girl was rude and disrespectful, and over a period of time, God healed Louise's heart. The time she spent on the church worship team was a beautiful experience *because* she made the right choices in an uncomfortable situation. Sadly, soon after that the girl left the church, but Louise learned several valuable lessons.

First of all, the enemy will use people to goad us—not just strangers on the street, but people who are very close to us, even spouses, relatives, or church family. In addition, the enemy can use *us* to goad others. It is hard to admit that our attitudes and feelings can be used to trip up other Christians, but it is true. The key here is in understanding that the enemy can only use us or abuse us if we allow him to. We must make difficult choices in every situation. We must choose to walk in love and take the high road. We must choose to hold our tongue in spite of words spoken against us. We must choose to be like Christ and lay down our personal good for the good of others.

Based on everything we have said so far, we are going to make a bold statement. It is our belief that one of the biggest misconceptions in the church today is that God is in charge. Yes, He *does* have a plan for our lives. It is a good and perfect plan, but

He has given us free will and authority over our own lives. This means ultimately we are responsible for every decision we make. God tells us in Matthew 16:19, "Whatever *you* bind is bound. Whatever *you* loose is loosed." In other words, whatever we do on earth affects heaven, which means if we do nothing, heaven can do nothing.

It is our legal right, as well as our responsibility, to use God's authority here on the earth. Instead, Christians stand back and watch Satan take advantage of our brothers and sisters in Christ. We do nothing, and they do nothing. It is as if we have forgotten, if we ever really knew, who we are in Christ and what we have because of Him. Remember that God has placed His Word even above Himself (Psalm 138:2). He will not break His word. God's word is His covenant. Whatever He says is so.

A missionary friend of Sandra's was getting ready to leave the country, but at the last minute he ran into problems with his papers. Because of the delay, it appeared that he would not be able to get the paper work he needed in time to make his flight. After several phone calls, he was told there was no way that the papers would arrive in time. Sandra prayed with him over the telephone, and they took authority over the situation. They commanded those papers to rise to the top of the stack and asked God to move on the hearts of the people in charge of processing the papers. They prayed in agreement, believing that God had already answered their prayers. Sure enough, the *very next* day, the papers were delivered and the missionary received phone calls from two different officials checking to make sure he had received them. It was a miracle. Some people would call it a coincidence, but we have experienced these types of occurrences with God over and over, and we know there are no coincidences in His kingdom.

Too many times, Christians just accept things the way they are instead of taking their authority and handing their circumstances over to God. For some reason they are under the impression that they should not bother God with their needs. We can see in God's Word that, because of Jesus, legal authority to dominate this earth was given back to mankind. We are called to rule and rein over every force of the enemy and take captive everything that is not of God. He says in His Word that the anointing is to *destroy yokes* and *remove burdens*. As we said earlier, if you are a Christian, you carry His anointing. God has given you the authority to stop every work of the enemy.

We want to take this opportunity to clear up some confusion in the church regarding the binding and loosing that is spoken of in Matthew 16:19. We believe, according to the Word, that Christians have the authority (given to us by Jesus and His work at the cross) to bind the works of the enemy (demons) and loose people who are bound in sin by preaching the Word to them. As far as binding Satan goes, only the Lord God Almighty has that privilege. But not to worry, his time is coming soon!

CHAPTER FIVE

SPEAKING TO THE WIND

A few years ago, we were invited to speak at a women's retreat outside of Anchorage, Alaska. Since we live in different states, we decided to meet in the Salt Lake City airport and then fly on to Alaska together. Upon our arrival in Salt Lake City, we discovered all flights to Anchorage had been cancelled due to hurricane force winds. Instead of being defeated by the weather, we immediately took authority over the situation and began quoting scripture to one another. We spent the entire day at the airport praying and refusing to accept the circumstances as they were. We believed it was God's will for us to speak at the retreat, and He was not going to let this ploy of the enemy keep us from it. Later that evening we learned Anchorage was going to open the airport just long enough for one airplane—*our* airplane—to land. They closed the airport to all flights after our plane landed. Once again, God confirmed to us the power we have when we take authority over *every* situation.

The story does not end there. As God often does, He rewarded us for our faithfulness with a special surprise. Because our flight had been delayed and our arrival into Anchorage was late at night, as we drove away from the airport, we were treated to a spectacular view of the Northern Lights. The wind was blowing all around us, but when we pulled the car over to the side of the road, it was like we were surrounded by a calm bubble. We were able to get out of the car and watch the wonderful show God had put on for us. It is no surprise that God works this way. Hebrews 11:6 tells us, "He is the rewarder of those who diligently seek Him."

We need to act with authority even when we do not feel like we are in control. In fact, we need to act with authority *especially* when we feel power-less. Remember that our authority is based on *God's Word* and our belief in it, not on how we feel about a situation, and He tells us He has not given us the spirit of fear, but of power, love and a sound mind (2 Timothy 1:7). A perfect example of this is when Jesus and the disciples were in a boat out on the Sea of Galilee. Jesus had fallen asleep when a brutal storm came up out of nowhere. The disciples were terrified, and when they woke Him up, He said, "Where is your faith?" In other words, "Why did you wake me instead of handling this yourselves?"

In another example, Paul talks about having a "thorn in his flesh" put there as a messenger by Satan. It was from Satan, *not from God*! Three times Paul cried out to God to do something. God did not say, "I know Paul, but remember that my grace is sufficient for *you* to suffer through." Instead He said, "My grace is sufficient for you." He was telling Paul He had already given him the authority, strength and grace to handle it. God desires us to understand the same thing today. He has already done what needs to be done; now we must walk in the authority. He has given us the keys; now we must use them.

As we have mentioned, God has given us the legal authority here on the earth. When we operate within our legal rights, it gives God permission to operate on our behalf. Remember, because man is a spirit in a body, humans are the only ones that can legally function here in the earth realm. Even demons must have a human body to operate here. When you fully understand this, you will begin to view prayer differently. You will begin to see prayer from a legal aspect. This will release you from getting caught up in the emotional roller coaster so many Christians associate with prayer. Our emotions are unstable and are prone to betray us. Thankfully, God says, "Whatever you *ask* in My name, I will do it." He did not say, "Whatever you *feel* in my name." In our ministry, we have witnessed some of the greatest healings when we did not feel a thing, because it is not about us. We did nothing but take our authority and believe God's covenant.

It is important to be reminded that since man is the legal authority on the earth, nothing happens without his active or passive permission. God will not violate His Word, and as such, He must get the agreement and cooperation of man. The Word says, "For the eyes of the Lord run to and fro throughout the whole earth to show Himself strong on behalf of those whose heart is loyal to Him" (2 Chronicles 16:9). He is always looking for someone to agree with Him. This is the reason Jesus instructed us to pray this way: "Our Father which art in heaven, hallowed be thy name, thy kingdom come, thy will be done *on earth* as it is in heaven." Prayer is giving God the legal right and permission to interfere in earthly affairs.

Unfortunately, Satan has deceived many of us into believing *he* has the power when, in fact, we do. He has convinced us that whatever happens, we just have to deal with it or live with it. On the contrary, Jesus says, "Behold I give you the authority to trample on serpents and scorpions, and *over all the power of the enemy*, and nothing shall by any means hurt you" (Luke 10:19). We cannot allow Satan to deceive us and rob us of our power and authority any longer. We must change the way we see ourselves in addition to the way we see the enemy. It is time to stand up and say, "Satan, in the name of Jesus, you are no longer going to influence my household or anything that concerns me."

CHAPTER SIX

GOOD OL' PETER

There are two elements of faith. One is believing that God can—that He has the ability; but then you must also believe that He has *given you* that power. Chapter 14 of the Gospel of Matthew tells us a story that so beautifully illustrates both of these elements.

> Immediately, Jesus made His disciples get into the boat and go before Him to the other side, while He sent the multitudes away. And when He had sent the multitudes away, He went up on the mountain by Himself to pray. Now when evening came, He was alone there. But the boat was now in the middle of the sea, tossed by the waves for the wind was contrary. Now in the fourth watch of the night, Jesus went to them walking on the sea. And when the disciples saw Him walking on

the sea, they were troubled saying, "It's a ghost," and they cried out for fear. But immediately, Jesus spoke to them saying, "Be of good cheer, it is I. Do not be afraid." (In Aramaic, *It is I* means *I Am*.) And Peter answered Him and said, "Lord if it is you, command me to come to you on the water." So He said, "Come."

This is so powerful that we need to take a closer look. So many of us have read this story a thousand times, and we have a whitewashed, Sunday school version that we take for granted. This compelling story goes far beyond the simple miracle of walking on water.

At the beginning of the story, it is early evening and we see Jesus send his disciples out in their boat while He stays behind to finish things up and pray. The Word says Jesus walked out to them in the fourth watch of the night, which puts it between three and six in the morning. Jesus had told them to go to the other side before dark, and now it was early morning and they still had not crossed the sea because of the contrary winds. The trip should only have taken two hours, but they had been at it all night and were getting nowhere. They were out in the middle of the sea, about to drown, bailing water and fighting for their lives. They could not overcome this storm. Then, just as all hope seemed to be lost, Jesus stepped onto the water and walked out over the top of the very situation that was about to kill his disciples.

When Jesus stepped out onto the water, it was the first time that had ever been done. This shows us we must trust that it is possible He will do something we have never seen before. He was totally in control. He was not upset or scared. The Bible does not mention hesitation or worry. We do not see Jesus wringing his hands and wondering if he is capable of walking on water. *Nothing* is too big for Jesus, which means nothing is too big for His Father in heaven. Sickness and disease are not too big for God to handle. Money issues, relationships, lawsuits, car trouble, child support payments—Jesus is fully capable of walking over the top of any storm that comes into our lives.

In addition, the disciples had no need to worry as they were walking in obedience. Jesus told them to go out in their boat, and we must not think for a second that the storm came as a surprise to Him. Sometimes God asks us to do difficult things that seem as hopeless as steering a boat across the sea in a raging storm. What we need to remember is that while we are steering in obedience, He is standing right beside us encouraging us to be of good cheer.

This story is also recounted in the gospel of Mark. In that version, the Bible says, "He (Jesus) came walking on the sea and *would have passed them by*." So many of us are so busy making a fuss about our problems as Jesus casually strolls along on the sea. Nothing bothers Him. He does not struggle and wonder how to solve our problems. The Lord had the answer long before we had the problem. Jeremiah 1:17 tells us that our Lord God made the heavens and the earth by His power and that *nothing* is too difficult for Him.

So, Jesus is walking on the water and the disciples are frightened, thinking they were seeing a ghost. Jesus calls to them and tells them, "Do not be afraid, it is I." So good ol' Peter, who is always putting his foot in his mouth, says in Matthew 14:28, "Lord, if it is you, command me to come to you on the water." We often get ourselves in trouble by asking too many questions, or worse, we ask the wrong questions. Peter did not ask the Lord if it was possible for him to walk on the water. He did not ask if it was God's will to walk on the water. He did not ask Jesus if he had enough faith to walk on the water, or even if he *should* walk on the water. Instead Peter said, "If it is you, command me to come to you," and so Jesus told him to come. There really was no reason for Peter to walk on the water, but Peter got his miracle when he stepped out onto the sea. Unfortunately, it did not last.

Verse 30 says, "But when he saw that the wind was boisterous, he was afraid. And beginning to sink, he cried out saying, 'Lord, save me,' and immediately Jesus stretched out His hand and caught him and said to him, 'Oh, ye of little faith. Why did you doubt?'"

So, in this story, Peter said to the Lord, "Give me Your word and I'll walk on the water," and the Lord told him to come, but He did not pick Peter up and *make* him walk on the water. Jesus did not grab Peter, pull him out of the boat and force him to walk on the water. The Lord simply told Peter to come, and Peter, *through faith*, got out of the boat. When the Lord said come, Peter believed that he had the ability to walk on the water. Peter is the one who got out of the boat. He is the one who took the steps. Peter is the one who started walking. He took action and did something supernatural by stepping out.

It is important to note that it was not God's will for Peter to walk only part way and then sink down, but when Peter took his eyes off Jesus and looked at the circumstances surrounding him, he began to sink. Some people believe that if God is really involved in something, it will just work. Well, God had to be involved with Peter walking on the water or he could not have done it, and yet, Peter began to sink. The truth is that God was *inspiring* him and *empowering* him, and faith was flowing *through* Peter, but when Peter took his eyes off Jesus, he *began* to sink. He did not sink suddenly, the way a brick sinks in a bathtub. He *began* to sink. It was a slow process; little by little the water came up over his ankles, and then up to his knees, as he began to sink. This mirrors Peter's faith. His faith did not disappear suddenly; it began to wane as Peter looked at all the other things going on around him. Once Peter took his eyes off the source of his power, he became distracted from his faith and that power stopped working as it should. Does this mean it was not God's power that caused him to walk on the water in the first place? This is a common misconception. There are some people who, after getting healed, when some of the symptoms come back, think it was not God after all. They believe if it truly were God, they would not have any more problems.

Another misconception is that God just does things without us. He does not do things without us; He flows through us. Jesus gave the command to come, but then Peter had to mix his obedience with his faith, take authority, and step out of the boat. When Peter stepped out, the power of God began to flow, but when fear crept in and he mentally and spiritually climbed back in the boat, he began to sink. The power started to subside. This did not happen because God changed, or because His Word changed. It started to subside because Peter changed. This takes us back to the point we made earlier. God does not do things *for* us—He has given us authority, dominion, and power. God flows through people, and He does not flow without us. In error we pray, "Oh God, we ask for Your healing," and then we just sit back and wait for God to do His thing. Since God flows through people, it is up to us to stand up and start taking our authority, rebuking things that are not of God and commanding situations to change. This is not disrespectful; this is taking hold of God's promises, His covenant, and being obedient to what the Word says. We believe the number one reason people do not receive is because they do not ask. They think it is enough to simply believe God has the power and ability to do the job.

Peter believed Jesus had the power to walk on water. If Peter did not believe, he would not have called out to Jesus for help when he began to sink. If he believed that this was a spirit and not Jesus, he would have yelled back to the men in the boat to save him. But he did not. He called out to Jesus. While Peter believed that Jesus could walk on water, he still found himself starting to sink. He started sinking because just believing that *Jesus* can do it is *not* faith. It is not enough to believe that Jesus could do it. We must believe what Jesus said: "The same works that I do, you shall do also." Our prayers need to be, "Father, I believe not only that You can do it, but I thank You that You gave *me* authority over all circumstances. Thank you for giving *me* power and dominion over Satan and his evil works, and I praise you that I can do all things through Your strength and by Your power and ability."

If we fail to take that second step and recognize our power and authority in Christ, we may as well not believe Jesus can do it, for all the good it will do us. The reason we are not seeing more manifestations of the power of God has nothing to do with God's willingness to release His power, and it is certainly not because we have not asked Him enough. We know God doesn't change with situations because the Bible tells us God is the same yesterday, today and forever. We believe the reason we are not seeing more manifestations of the power of God is because there are just not enough people who know their position in Christ.

If we do not know, or we fail to understand what we have, then we cannot fully use it. That is the way it is with many Christians. We cry out to God, saying, "Oh God, I'm asking you to pour out Your power." According to the scriptures, we have already been given the same power that raised Christ from the dead. It is living inside us, and yet here we are, asking for more power. What more can God give us—what more can He do? In spite of the fact that the Bible says we have the same faith Jesus had, we make the mistake of thinking we need more faith. The point here is, God has *already done His part*. He has already given us everything we need to be victorious in this life. We need to believe that instead of heading *to* victory, we are coming *from* victory. We need to stop trying to obtain victory and realize we already have it in Christ. It is time for Christians to rise up, believe what the Word of God says, and stop begging God to answer our prayers. Instead, we need to listen for His voice, put our eyes on Him, obey His commands, and *get out of the boat*!

CHAPTER SEVEN

FAITH, FAITH, AND MORE FAITH

The Bible says in Galatians 3:11 that "…the just shall live by faith." As Christians, it should be our greatest desire to please God, but Hebrews 11 tells us that without faith it is impossible to do so. The very definition of faith is to have an unquestioning belief in God, a complete trust and reliance on Him without proof or evidence. For most people, seeing is believing, but with God, believing is seeing. Hebrews 11 goes on to tell us that, "Faith is the substance of things hoped for, the evidence of things not seen." The very force that brings into manifestation that for which you believe is called faith. Faith is the confident assurance that what we hope for is going to happen. It is the evidence of things we cannot yet see. We can only accomplish the impossible when we see the invisible. This is a law of the universe. That is why God says it is impossible to please Him without it. The question, then, is how do we get faith?

When we give our hearts to Jesus and become new creations in Christ, God gifts us with a supernatural faith. It is not our faith, but rather the faith of God. It is the same faith Jesus had, and the Bible tells us it comes by hearing. We cannot believe unless we hear God's Word—not just with our ears, but with our hearts as well. Faith—found in God's Word—unlocks our understanding of scripture while releasing God's Spirit to be active in our lives. Through faith we can approach God boldly to receive His promises. Since faith is based on the knowledge of God's Word and His character, the more we get to know God and the more intimate our relationship with Him becomes, the more our faith grows. It is one of the key points to operating in His kingdom. That is why God wants us to read the Bible and spend time with Him every day. Not only does He desire that intimacy with us, but also He desires that we get to know Him and how He operates so that we can cooperate with Him. God is limited in what He can do for us by our knowledge of His promises. While He loves us, and wants to do great things for us, we choose how much He blesses our lives by learning His promises and exercising our faith.

Faith is like a muscle in our body. The more we use it, the stronger it becomes. We never actually receive additional faith, but the faith we have grows and gets stronger. Like our muscles, if we fail to exercise our faith, it will grow weak and useless. Along those same lines, if we try to lift too much for the strength we have, we will strain ourselves. Faith is much the same way. It is foolishness to attempt to believe God for something big if we have never trusted Him for the small things, such as a pair of socks or a loaf of bread. The time to exercise our faith is not when we are in the middle of a trial, but every day, starting small and working on it every day. We can begin with simple things like asking God to help us find something that has been misplaced, or asking for help with a difficult task.

It is important for us to remember to be grateful and thank Him when we see the results. These little things might seem insignificant, but even the smallest answers from God are faith builders and the more we use our faith, the stronger it will become. We cannot study God's Word to get more faith, but we can study it to learn how faith operates. It is not that we have a lack of faith; it is that we have an abundance of unbelief.

Some people use only a little of the faith God gives them. Others believe God for greater things and receive them. When you attempt great things for God, you honor Him. This is not arrogance; it is confidence in the promises of God. His Word is true. The point is to use your faith all the time and for all situations. As believers, we have the faith to overcome any obstacle.

Several years ago Sandra's friend Linda, a Christian single mother, was running out of toilet paper.

Money was tight, and she still had several days until payday. Out of desperation, she sat down and began to pray. She told God that her family needed toilet paper. At the same time that she was informing God of her need, Sandra, who was shopping at Wal-Mart and completely unaware of Linda's prayers across town, was suddenly impressed to buy Linda toilet paper. The next morning at church Sandra leaned over to Linda and told her to pull her car around after the service because Sandra had something for her. As Sandra opened the trunk, Linda began to cry and explained that she had prayed for this very gift just the day before. Within minutes, our pastor came over and asked her to pull her car over near his because he had a station wagon full of toilet paper for her. That was eight years ago at the time of this writing, and God is still continuing to bless her with toilet paper.

This little story shows us that nothing is too overwhelming or too insignificant for God. If it is our need, it is all-important to Him. We are His children and He loves us so much. He is concerned with everything that concerns us. His word says that He numbers the hairs on our head!

What a mighty, loving Father God He is! We are His children. He wants to help us with our lives and it gives Him pleasure to bless us. He has already made provision for *more* than everything that we could ever need long before the need ever arises. All we need to do is believe.

Not long ago, Louise's car died. It was beyond repair, so Louise began to pray for a car to replace her old one. In the meantime, she had to drive her husband's big SUV. To make matters even worse, they lived twenty-five miles from town, and the gas mileage was horrible. Louise hated it! She went from driving her cozy, comfortable car to this giant beast of a thing that seemed to swallow her up.

While dressing to go to town one morning, God began to work on Louise's heart regarding her faith. Louise had no doubt that God would provide another vehicle—a newer used car, maybe two or three years old—but as God spoke to her heart, she began to realize that instead of asking God for the least He could provide, she should believe Him for a brand new car. The more she thought about it, the more she believed it. She began to change her thinking and the way she was praying. She began to thank God for the new and perfect car He was going to provide.

Later that afternoon, Louise was still praying and thanking God when she took her husband's car and headed for town. By the time she had traveled the several miles to the main road, she knew without a doubt that God had a brand new car for her. Her faith took hold, and she drove all over town excited about the new car that was coming. Within three weeks, God had worked an incredible miracle and Louise was driving a brand new car, *paid in full.* The lesson here is that we should not go to God asking Him for the least that we think He will give us. He is a generous and loving God who wants to bless His children with the best gifts He has. If we seek Him first and exercise our faith, He will be faithful to provide us with all that we ask and more.

CHAPTER EIGHT

FAITH VERSUS FEAR

Now that we have discussed faith, we must address fear. Like faith, fear is also a force. But fear does not come from God, and is in direct opposition to faith. Second Timothy tells us that God has not put fear in our hearts. Fear comes from the enemy of our soul. Satan takes that force of fear and uses it to manifest what we are afraid of. All of us are afraid of different things: death, loss, illness, war, poverty, punishment, being alone, the future, and the unknown. For some of us, our fear can be paralyzing.

Several years ago, Louise had a sore shoulder. She had heard so many horror stories regarding cortisone shots that she was afraid to go the doctor. Finally, the pain got so bad that her shoulder froze and she had no choice but to go. Of course, as soon as she got into the examination room, the doctor informed her that she would need to have a shot of cortisone. Her fear was being realized, and when he left the room to get the shot, Satan began to build on that seed of fear.

By the time he returned, her heart was pounding so fast she thought she might have a heart attack. She was beside herself and on the verge of tears. The doctor numbed her shoulder and then gave her the shot. She never felt a thing. All that worry and fear was for nothing, but because she had not taken care of the shoulder to begin with, she ended up needing six months of physical therapy in addition to the shot of cortisone. Louise cried more and endured more pain in those six months than if she had just faced her fear and asked for the shot in the first place. It was a valuable lesson.

God knew that we would have to deal with this enemy many times in our lives, and He gave us hundreds of scriptures to help us deal with fear. In Psalm 27:1-3 (NLT), David declares, "The Lord is my light and my salvation, so why should I be afraid? The Lord protects me from danger, so why should I tremble? When evil people come to destroy me, when my enemies and foes attack me, they will stumble and fall. Though a mighty army surround me, my heart will know no fear. Even if they attack me, I remain confident." He continues on in verse five, "For he will conceal me there when troubles come; He will hide me in His sanctuary. He will place me out of reach on a high rock."

David had the right attitude. He had such confidence in his Lord that fear could not overtake him. Like David, we need to believe that God will protect us and always cause us to triumph if we keep our faith in Him. In Proverbs 3:25-26 (NLT) we are reminded, "You need not be afraid of disaster or the destruction that comes upon the wicked, for the Lord is your security. He will keep your foot from being caught in a trap."

One cold November morning several years ago, Louise's husband, Pete, woke her in the middle of the night, saying that he was feeling ill. When she turned on the light, she could see that his color was very bad and she immediately called an ambulance. Upon arriving at the hospital, the emergency room staff hooked him up to heart monitors and then asked Louise to stay in the waiting room. Things seemed fine until a nurse came out and informed Louise that Pete was having a heart attack and they were working to stabilize him.

At first Louise sat in disbelief because Pete was so young, and in his fifty-two years, he had rarely ever been sick. As fear began to set in, a doctor came to tell her that while Pete was stabilized, the next twenty-four hours would determine if he lived or died. Louise was in shock as she called her children, and then, of course, she called Sandra. Sandra was as surprised as Louise, but had the presence of mind to quote the last verse of the ninety-first Psalm, which says, "With long life will I satisfy him, and show him my salvation" (KJV). Louise stood on that promise, and as she prayed, she reminded God that Pete was not satisfied yet, that he had not had a long life, and she and Pete both needed God to step in and show them His salvation.

Pete not only made it through that initial twenty-four hours, but also after seven days he was released from the hospital. The amazing thing is that because he had suffered his heart attack in the hospital, they were able to treat him with a new medicine that had only been available for a little over a month. That, however, was not the end of the trouble. Once home, he began to experience negative symptoms, and Louise rushed him back to the hospital. This time the doctors attempted to perform angioplasty, a procedure in which they open arteries with balloons. After five unsuccessful tries, the doctor came to Louise with less than encouraging news. He informed her that he was going to make one more attempt, but that would be all he could do.

Louise took her authority and began to pray and quote God's Word over the situation. The doctor returned with good news. The procedure had worked and Pete was doing well. Not only was he thriving, but also within a relatively short period of time, his heart was completely healed. He has had several tests since then, and one doctor refused to believe that Pete had ever had a heart attack. We believe we received a real miracle because we chose to stand on God's promises from the very first moments of trouble instead of caving in to fear and doubt.

The choice is ours in every situation. Over and over we are told that we have been delivered from all fear, but will we believe God, or will we listen to our enemy? We must choose whether to exercise our faith or give in to our fear. Fear gets us nowhere; we worry and obsess about what *might* come our way, and we are overcome with negative thoughts. Once we have given power to those negative thoughts, we have made the way for desperation and hopelessness to sweep right in. We must train ourselves to walk in faith and to rebuke fear. It takes some practice but it can be done. It is so much better to walk in faith, believe God's promises, and leave no room for the negative thoughts of fear. This is why God tells us to take control of our thoughts in the tenth chapter of Second Corinthians. He says, "We must bring every thought into captivity to the obedience of Christ."

In Philippians 4:8, He gives us a very detailed list of the things on which we should be focusing our thoughts. "...Whatsoever things are true, whatsoever things are honest, whatsoever things are just, whatsoever things are pure, whatsoever things are lovely, whatsoever things are of good report, if there be any virtue or if there be any praise, think on these things." Here God has given us a checklist to help us evaluate each of our thoughts. We can examine them one at a time based on their Greek translations.

The word *true* means *actual*. We must ask ourselves if our thought is accurate—if it is truth. The word *honest* means *honorable*, and we must make sure that our thoughts will honor God. The word *just* means *right* or *righteous*, and as a result, we must check that our thoughts line up with the only righteousness, the Word of God. The word *pure* means *uncontaminated*, which means we must take care that our motivation has not been tainted with selfishness or pride. The word *lovely* means *pleasing*, and of course, we want all of our thoughts to please God. *Good report* is translated to mean *said of things kindly, graciously*, so we must ask ourselves if our thoughts will reflect on others kindly and graciously. The word *virtue* means *moral excellence*, so we must check to make sure that our thoughts are above reproach. Last, but definitely not least, the word *praise* means *praiseworthy*, which reminds us that every thought should glorify God.

We must learn to control our thoughts and keep them on the things of God. Someone once said, "You cannot stop the birds from flying over your head, but you can stop them from nesting in your hair!" We must put a guard on our minds so we can think of the things God wants us thinking on and reject every thought that does not line up with God's Word. The only way that change will come is if we train ourselves to pay attention to what we are thinking. We must be quick to realize when we let our minds wander off track and then swiftly pull our thoughts back in line with what God says. Our goal should be to try to think the way God thinks. We can encourage ourselves by remembering all the things He has done for us in the past.

Unfortunately, there will always be someone who will try to discourage us; someone always wants to rain on our parade, especially if we are thinking big. Psalm 105:5 tells us to "remember His marvelous works which He has done." Anyone who has been a Christian for more than five minutes has something about which to be encouraged. When we remember what He has done for us in the past, our faith is built and we are encouraged and excited about the future. This is also a great weapon to use against the enemy when he comes to whisper lies in our ears. This is why it is so important for us to think before we speak. This is also why, as we mentioned before, God tells us to think on things that are true, honest, just, pure, lovely, of good report, virtuous and praiseworthy; He knew we needed a guide and that is exactly what He gave us in His Word. When we follow this plan, He will be with us and give us His peace. Sadly, what most of us do is exactly the opposite.

An example of this would be a situation in which a person hears that his company is going to lay off some people in his department. He is in his car driving home, and the thought comes into his mind that he could be one of them. Suddenly, he is gripped with fear. He starts thinking that he could lose his house and his car. From there he moves to worrying about having enough money to feed his family. He begins to panic because he is seeing only the problem. By the time he gets home, his blood pressure is up and he is very worried and fearful. It is a downward spiral. Now he takes his fear and worries and passes them on to his wife by telling her all the negative details. So before anything has actually come to pass, two people are living in fear. What we need to do, when presented with the choice, is focus on what God has promised for our lives and see the situation as an opportunity to exercise our faith.

There was a time when Sandra had just such an opportunity. She had quit her job to take a better position elsewhere. Unfortunately, at the last minute the new position fell through and all of a sudden, she had no job. She had never had any trouble finding employment, so she was confident that another job would be hers right away. Much to her surprise, it did not happen that way and in no time, she had used up her unemployment benefits and her savings and now, in addition to not having a job, she had no money for the first time in her life. Fear tried to take over her thoughts, but her faith in God's promises would not allow it.

This went on for three months. Looking back, Sandra can see how God provided for her every day as she looked to Him instead of the circumstances around her. Miraculous things began to happen. For instance, at a time when Sandra did not know how she was going to pay the rent at the end of two weeks, a friend in another state heard of her situation and sent a card containing three hundred dollars.

Sandra was overjoyed and called her to thank her and to praise God for His faithfulness. In the course of the conversation, she mentioned that the check was half of her rent. That evening the friend told her husband about the situation and he told her to send the other half. A week later, the second check arrived and Sandra had her rent money a week before she even needed it. Many similar things happened in those three months. The unemployment office found money in a special program and sent two hundred dollars. The electric company sent two hundred and eighty five dollars as a refund of an overpayment on a billing balance. God was so faithful that Sandra was never late on a bill or missed a meal, or did without in any way.

Finally, one day Sandra was looking out the window and asking God why she had been without a job all this time. A few days later she went to a job interview and found out. She was offered the job as the office manager for an optometrist's new practice. The entire time that Sandra had been trusting God to provide, and wondering what was taking so long, the doctor had been building his offices. When the office was completed, Sandra had the job she had believed for, and it was right around the corner from home. In fact, it was in the same direction as the window she had been looking out just days before. You see, if Sandra had allowed fear and doubt to move in, the outcome would have been much different. The circumstances we find ourselves in are not as important as the choices we make regarding our attitude toward them. The outcome will be greatly influenced by whether we choose to believe God and the things He has spoken, or the enemy and the lies he plants in our minds. We need to remember that the only power the enemy has is the power we give him.

We cannot emphasize enough the need to trust God in every situation. He knows your needs and His timing is always perfect. A few years back, Sandra believed God to be debt free by the end of the year. As the months went by, every time she had extra money, she paid off a bill. She was doing her part and trusting God to do His. By the first of December, seven hundred dollars of her debt was still outstanding and it looked as though her year-end goal was not going to be met. Sandra had to fight doubt and unbelief as each day passed. She quoted God's Word and tried not to dwell on her doubts. She continued to focus on what God said even though it seemed hopeless. The battle was difficult because the enemy would try to tell her that God was not going to come through for her, or that she had not heard God correctly. Satan tried many different ways to steal her faith, but she continued to stand on the Word of God.

On December 23, just as Sandra was preparing to leave work for the Christmas break, her boss handed her a Christmas card which contained a bonus check in the amount of seven hundred dollars. Not only was she able to pay off her debt completely, but she did so with over a week to spare. The world would tell us that this was a coincidence, but we believe that there are no coincidences in the kingdom of God. Everything is part of His perfect plan and everything is according to His perfect timing.

CHAPTER NINE

POWER-PACKED
PRAYERS

There is an old song that says prayer is the key to heaven, but faith unlocks the door. Remember—faith is what unleashes God's power to manifest the answers to our prayers here on earth. The spirit of the world is in direct opposition to the Spirit of God, but when we determine to stand in faith, the world loses any controlling influence over us. The Bible tells us in 1 John 5:14-15, "Now this is the confidence that we have in Him, that if we ask anything according to His will, He hears us. And if we know that He hears us, whatever we ask, we know that we have the petitions that we have asked of Him." This scripture assures us we can ask God for anything according to His will. In addition, the Gospel of John tells us to use the name of Jesus when we pray. Prayer offered in the name of Jesus is in accord with His revealed nature and purpose. It has the full weight of His authority behind it. We are to be commanders, not beggars. God has already provided every thing we need; we simply need to command it to be manifested. All things are given by grace and we receive all things by faith. His Word says that we are to walk in divine health, living abundant lives, having all our needs met. We should have more than enough in every area of our lives.

The sixth chapter of Ephesians illustrates perseverance in prayer. Moses prayed for forty days for the deliverance of Israel. Elijah prayed seven times for rain. As Christians, we have no business giving up. Sometimes our answers are simply in transit, and we should never take a chance that we are giving up just the moment before our answer arrives.

Several years ago, when Sandra's family lived in California, her oldest son Steve and his wife decided to move out of the state. For whatever reason, they chose to withdraw from the family, and without telling anyone where they went, they took Sandra's only grandchild and disappeared. For the first few months, she cried a river of tears. One day while she was in the shower crying, she realized that this was too much of a burden to carry any longer, so she prayed and asked God to restore her family. In the natural, it did not look possible, but she was determined to stand in faith for as long as it took. From then on, she thanked God for the restoration of her family. As the enemy so often does, he would whisper in her ear negative things like, "Maybe they are all dead," or, "You will never see your grandson again." When that would happen, Sandra would repeat God's promise to restore her family. She would remind herself that nothing was impossible with Him. This went on for many years—six and one half years, to be exact. During that time, Sandra left California and moved to Spokane, Washington. Once she moved, the enemy tried to convince her that Steve would never be able to find her now, even if he wanted to.

One Sunday morning in March, several months after Sandra had moved, she had a dream that she was sitting on a blanket at the beach and there was a telephone on the blanket next to her. The phone rang and when she picked it up she heard, "Hello Mom, this is Steve." The dream shocked her and she woke up with a start, but she knew immediately that it was God letting her know that He was getting ready to restore her family. She had never experienced God in this way, but she knew that God was about to move. She was so sure of it, in fact, that she told everyone in her Sunday school class about the dream. She wanted them to know what was about to happen ahead of time, so that when it did happen, it would build their faith too. It was in March of that year.

Two months later, Louise came to visit Spokane over Memorial Day weekend. We traveled all over the area exploring and ended up in Coeur d'Alene, Idaho, at the park near the lake. Since we were only forty-five minutes from Spokane, we decided to go home and start fresh the next day. The next morning, we were sitting in Sandra's living room having our coffee when the phone rang. When she picked up the receiver, she heard, "Hello Mom, this is Steve."

It turned out that he was living in Coeur d'Alene, Idaho, and had no idea that Sandra had moved to Washington until someone had recently told him. In addition, Steve and his family had been at the same park at the same time as Sandra and Louise the day before. God had a plan, and it was not for a family reunion in the park. The plan was for Sandra's family to be restored as she had been shown, with a phone call. During the time that Sandra was clinging to her faith in God's promises and refusing to believe the lies of the enemy, God was busy working out details so that not only would Sandra's family be restored, but also her son and grandson would end up living just down the road. The lesson here is that we should never give up. We never know when our miracle might be just around the corner.

As important as it is for us to pray and believe, many Christians find it difficult to pray. They are self-conscious and wonder if they are "doing it right." Mathew 6:6 in the Message Bible says, "Here's what I want you to do, find a quiet, secluded place so you will not be tempted to role-play before God. Just be there as simply and honestly as you can manage. As you do this the focus will shift from you to God, and you will begin to sense His presence." We need to stop worrying about having the right words come out of our mouths, because He is listening to our hearts. We can tell Him briefly about our problem, but there is no need to go into every detail; He already knows the details. What He wants is for us to repeat back to Him the scripture that is the solution to our problems. In Isaiah 43:26, God instructs us to put Him in remembrance of His word and to say, "Father, you said...." John 15:7-11 says, "If you abide in me and my words abide in you, you will ask what you desire and it shall be done for you. By this my Father is glorified, that you bear much fruit so you will be my disciples. These things I have spoken to you that my joy may remain in you and your joy may be full." The key word in this scripture is *abide*. God's Word has to live in us, in our hearts, in our minds, and in our mouths. Our prayers are the outcome of Christ's life in us. We should never be intimidated when we come before God because He wants us to be happy, and wants us to tell Him what we need. In addition, we should not be comparing the way we pray to the way others pray.

There was a time when Louise was in bible school that she, her husband, Pete, and Sandra were all living together. Pete and Sandra never wanted to pray over our meals because they thought Louise could pray better. So mealtime went like this: "You pray." "No, you pray." Then Louise would end up praying. What we did not realize at the time was that God hears any prayer offered by any person in the name of Jesus. One man might pray, "Oh, dear heavenly Father, sanctify this meal to our bodies and bless the hands that prepared it," while another man may say, "Hey, God, thanks for the grub." Both prayers are right and both prayers are heard because it is not about content; it is a matter of the heart.

Sometimes it might seem as though God does not always answer our prayers, but if we pray according to His Word and in the name of Jesus, He will always answer. What we must remember is that He may answer us differently than the way we want. Because He loves us so much, there might be a delay. He sees the big picture and we see only the small part in front of us. He is a wise father and He will not give us what we want if it is something that may harm us. Just as a wise parent would not give their toddler a gun with which to play, God, who sees far off, will only provide us with safe and good gifts. We must trust that He knows what is best for us, and this is where our faith comes in.

Sandra always ends her personal prayers with, "This is what I want, Lord, but if it is not what you have in mind, I want Your will, not mine." Jesus prayed this way when He was in the Garden of Gethsemane before the guards came to get Him. He was asking for God to release him from what was coming, but ultimately he said, "Nevertheless, Your will, not mine." God promises us in His Word that He will give us even more than what we pray for, so we should always want what He wants. Remember, we cannot out think God, because He is huge! Ephesians 3:20 tells us, "Now to Him who is able to do exceedingly abundantly above all that we ask or think, according to the power that works *in us*."

He never ceases to amaze us with the blessings He brings into our lives—not just the things that we pray for, but also other things that are so small we do not even bother to bring them to Him. Because He knows everything about us, He is aware of what we are longing for, and like any good parent, our awesome Father in heaven loves to give His children good gifts.

An example of this is a friend of ours who was craving turkey dinner with all the fixings. It was at the beginning of summer—nowhere near Thanksgiving—but she wanted turkey and dressing and even pumpkin pie. She could not justify fixing such a large dinner for herself, and no one else in her family was interested, so she just tried to ignore her desire and hold out until November. Sometime later, she was invited to dinner by some people in her church, and the hostess had decided to go all out and fix a turkey dinner, complete with dressing and pumpkin pie.

This is another situation in which the world would comment on the nice coincidence, but we would say that God put it on the heart of the cook to fix our friend's favorite meal. It is times like this that our friend sings a little song about how God loves her best, but of course we know our God loves us all best, and when we start paying attention to and looking for what God is doing in our lives, we begin to see that He meets even these little needs, all the time. He loves to bless us, and He has very unusual and creative ways to show His love. Just as parents love to see the look of surprise on the faces of their children, God loves us so much and delights in blessing us. We believe that if more Christians could fully understand this principal, our prayer lives would change dramatically.

CHAPTER TEN

PRAYER PLANTING

Once we have taken our needs to God in prayer, we must wait on Him. The key to successful waiting is patience. In other words, we must resist the wiggles. We should take our cue from the farmer. He does not plant on Monday and then come back and dig up the seed on Wednesday to see how it is coming along. He already knows that the seed planted will produce a harvest and his experience tells him that everything has a season. He faithfully weeds, waters and nurtures, knowing all the time that the seed is germinating and will produce a harvest in due season.

Prayer planting is exactly the same. When we pray we must believe that we have received according to Mark 11:24, which says, "Therefore I say to you, whatever things you ask when you pray, believe that you receive them, and you will have them." We are then assured of a crop, but we must remember that some seeds take longer to mature than others. This is where faith comes in. Ephesians 6:13 says, "Having done all, stand." What this means is that sometimes we will need to trust and believe in spite of the way circumstances appear.

In 1997, Louise and Pete retired and moved to Montana. They moved in with their children but believed that God would provide them with their own home. Finally, after three months, Louise became frustrated and took matters into her own hands. Getting ahead of God never works out well, but she searched the classified ads and found a duplex for rent. She went to check it out, and it was too small and not what they wanted. But she felt desperate, so she told the landlord that they would take it. Louise got in her car and cried all the way home, because she knew that this was not what God had for them. She had no peace in her spirit about renting it and after a sleepless night, she called the landlord and told him that she was sorry, but that they were not going to be able to rent the duplex after all.

A few days later, Louise attended a women's Bible study for the first time at her new church where she knew no one. When they asked for prayer requests, she saw her arm shoot up like she had no control over it. She began to share with them her need for a place to live and gave them her list of requirements. A young woman sitting across the room immediately caught her eye and whispered,

"I have a place for you." Louise was so excited that she could hardly wait for the meeting to be over so she could talk to the woman. As it turned out, she had been praying for a Christian couple to live in the empty house on their farm. At this writing, Pete and Louise have lived in that house for eight years. It is a perfect example of the "God who sees afar off and provides." They trusted God and He gave them even more that what they asked. They live out in the country on a beautiful farm, with horses and critters and everything they always wanted, and Pete is living his childhood dream. Their landlords have become their good friends, and they are continually blessing each other. Neuman Farm is their piece of heaven on earth.

Some seeds come up right away, while others take longer to mature. Sometimes, because human will is involved, God has to do a work in human hearts. Our job is to weed, water, nurture and wait. The Bible tells us in Genesis 8:22 that there is a time for seed and a time for harvest. This is another of God's principles and this law works for both good and bad seeds. Knowing that there will always be a harvest of some sort, we should always be focused on planting good seeds. There are all kinds of seeds. Among the good seeds are love, patience, kindness and generosity. These are the kind of crops we want to see growing in our lives. There are also bad seeds such as deceitfulness, jealousy, unfaithfulness and cruelness. These, too, will produce a crop, but obviously not the type we want. We choose what we plant, so we cannot be surprised at the crop that comes up.

Once we have prayed, no matter what happens, we must not be deceived by circumstances. We have to continue to believe in spite of the way things seem. Some people will call this denial, but that is because they do not understand that Christians operate differently. Remember, God tells us to live *in* the world but not *like* the world. We have to draw a line in the sand. Although circumstances are subject to change, our God *never* changes. He is always the same, yesterday, today and forever. Either we believe Him, or we do not.

One time we were in Italy and it was pouring down rain. We needed to go to the train station, and our hotel desk clerk told us we would not be able to get a cab because they were in such high demand. He had been trying to get a cab for someone else for almost two hours and they had finally taken a bus to the airport. He suggested that we could take our bags and walk two blocks in the downpour and *possibly*, we *might* be able to get a cab there. We immediately started to quietly call on the name of Jesus for help. Within minutes, the hotel manager came in the door and asked what the problem was. He pulled out his cell phone, made a call, said something in Italian, and while he was still on the phone, a cab pulled up to the door. We smiled at each other, knowing that because of Jesus, all circumstances are subject to change. We got to our train on time because we have learned how to cooperate with God.

Another important key to waiting on God is to stay out of His way. We must trust God to take care of things. Contrary to popular belief, He does not need our help. Look what happened to Abraham; God promised him a son. Abraham stood in faith for 25 years and then let Sarah talk him into "helping" God. Ishmael was born, and the Hebrew nation is still dealing with those consequences today. Imagine how much better it would have been had Abraham and Sarah listened to God and done it His way, instead of thinking that He needed their help.

The best way to nurture our prayers is to line up our mouths with what we have prayed. So many times, we have prayed with people only to have them contradict the prayer with negative words. Sometimes, we barely get "amen" out before unbelief comes out of their mouth. Mark 11:24 says that we must believe that we receive when we pray. If we really believe, we will not say anything that contradicts that prayer, we will not think anything that contradicts that prayer, and we will not acknowledge any circumstance that contradicts that prayer. Remember Paul's instructions in Ephesians 6:13, that "having done all, stand." Our part is standing; God will do His part.

CHAPTER ELEVEN

WHAT IS THE HOLDUP?

There are many things that hinder our prayers, but God is so good He even helps us with these. Psalm 66:18 says, "If I regard iniquity in my heart, the Lord will not hear." Iniquity means sin, and this can be anything from unforgiveness and disobedience to bitterness and anger. When we hide those things in our hearts, we stop the flow of God in our lives, and our prayers cannot be answered.

We once knew a woman who had received a very negative letter from her ex-son-in-law. She was so filled with unforgiveness and bitterness that she carried that letter in her purse for over a year. As much as God wanted to bless her, her unforgiveness stood in the way. Mark 11:25-26 tell us, "And whenever you stand praying, if you have anything against anyone, forgive him, that your Father in heaven may also forgive you your trespasses." Forgiveness is for *our* benefit and *our* relationship with God, even if the other person never knows anything about it. We have to forgive, even when we think we are right. It is not about being right; it is about being right with God.

In Matthew 18 Jesus refers to offenses. The Greek word used here is *scandalon*. It is a beautiful depiction of what offenses do to us. A *scandalon* is the part of a trap that sticks up in the middle, to hold the bait when trapping animals. It is the trigger of the trap. When the animal takes the bait, the *scandalon* snaps, and the animal is caught. Once trapped, it is nearly impossible to get free. That is how it is with our enemy; he sets the trap and loves it when we become caught in the offense. Often we take offense, and the other person has no idea he has offended us; he just goes on about his business leaving us there, stuck in the trap. What God wants is for us to become completely unaware of offense and keep our eyes on Him.

Sometimes iniquity refers to something smaller, such as jealousy, because someone else got a pat on the back at work and we did not. Or perhaps someone else receives the very thing you have been asking God for. These may seem like small things, but they are big hindrances to our prayers, because they get rooted deep in our hearts. Isaiah 59:1-2 tells us that if we will not confess and forsake our sins, He will not hear. Iniquity blocks our prayers, and we need to get right with God.

Being right with God is the most important thing. It is more important than being right with man. Sometimes when Louise gets mad at Pete, she has to go into another room and repent. She will ask God to change *her*—to make her more understanding, more loving. She does not ask Him to change Pete, as that is not her business. She cannot control what Pete says or does, but she can control her response, and in reality, we cannot even do that without God's help. God instructs us in 1 Peter 3:6-7 that if we honor our spouse and do not mistreat him or her, our prayers will not be hindered.

Sometimes our prayers are blocked by something that does not necessarily look like sin. In Proverbs 21:13 we see that, "Whoever shuts his ears to the cry of the poor will also cry himself and not be heard." God is saying here that it is a mandate to help the poor. Our own prayers will not be heard if we refuse to help those in need. Often we hear the old saying, "God helps those who help themselves," but please be advised that this is found *nowhere* in the Bible. The truth is that the Lord helps those who help *others*. No matter how little we have, someone else has less. We might not be able to help the whole world, but we should always be willing to fill a need when it is in our power to do so. Our Lord wants us to determine in our hearts to be a blessing and be looking for opportunities to bless. It never has to be something big; it could be as simple as putting money in an expired parking meter or taking a casserole to a new neighbor on moving day.

When we are willing, the Holy Spirit will show us opportunities to bless.

Recently, Louise was standing in line at a potluck dinner and noticed that a lady was headed towards the line using a walker. Louise had spotted a small plate of her very favorite deviled eggs but knew that if she got out of line to help the elderly woman, they would be gone by the time she returned to the line. It was a tough decision between her spirit and her flesh, but ultimately her spirit won. Louise not only helped the woman with her plate, but when she was seated, got her a beverage as well. When Louise got back into the line, she was pleased to find several of those delicious eggs waiting for her, and they tasted even better knowing that she had been obedient and served the woman as Jesus would have.

Unbelief is possibly the biggest hindrance to our prayers. There is a story in the Bible in the ninth chapter of Mark that tells of a father who brings his demon-possessed son to Jesus. In verse 23, Jesus says, "If you can believe, all things are possible." In verse 24, the father says, "Lord I believe. Help my unbelief." We must remember that we do not have a lack of faith, but an abundance of *unbelief*. When the two of us are praying with people during ministry time, we tell them up front that if they are having a problem with unbelief, we need to know. This way, we can start out by praying for their unbelief before we go on to pray for their need.

Jesus tells us in Mathew 18:18-19, "Assuredly, I say to you, whatever you bind on earth will be bound in heaven, and whatever you loose on earth will be loosed in heaven. Again I say to you that if two of you agree on earth concerning anything that they ask, it will be done for them by my father in heaven." This does not mean God will give us whatever we ask for. He is not Santa Claus. We must be asking according to the will of God. First John 5:14 (Amplified) says, "And this is the confidence (the assurance, the privilege of boldness) which we have in Him: (we are sure) that if we ask anything (make any request) according to His will (in agreement with His own plan), He hears us."

In addition, we must be praying with someone who is genuinely in agreement with our prayer. Many times when our prayer requests are not met, we blame God, when in reality, we may have been praying with someone who was not fully in agreement with us. It is important for us to choose our prayer partners wisely. By that same token, if we are asked to pray in agreement with someone and we know in our hearts that for whatever reason we cannot believe with them, we need to be honest and let them know, so they can find someone else to pray with.

Once we have prayed in agreement, it is not necessary to move from person to person, asking each one to agree with us for the same request. If we truly believe that our prayer has been heard, then we need to believe we have received and start expecting and praising God for the answer.

Last, but definitely not least, we must always put God first. Mark 6:32-33 tells us God knows all our needs, and if we first seek God and His righteousness, all of these needs will be met. Sadly these days, people get so busy. They fail to put God first, then they cannot understand why everything is so chaotic.

Ezekiel 14:3 says, "Men have set up their idols in their hearts and put before them that which causes them to stumble into iniquity." In other words, they put other things before God, and it caused them to fall into sin. Let us take for example the man who has been praying for a boat so he can take his family fishing. God has made the provision, but now he is taking his family fishing every weekend. Not only has he set up a stumbling block for himself (fishing, instead of church), but he is leading his family astray as well. The boat has become his idol. Does this mean no one should have a boat or go fishing? Absolutely not, but God must be our priority in every situation.

Louise recalls a time when she was sick on a Sunday and missed church. The following Sunday it was pouring down rain, and they could not get into town for church. Then something else came up the third Sunday, and suddenly she realized they had missed almost an entire month. That fourth Sunday, Louise made getting to church a priority, because in addition to missing service, she was also skipping some of her usual time with God as well. It is not that Louise was in sin, but she felt like she was slipping away. Proverbs 28:9 tells us, "If we neglect the Word of God, our prayers shall be an abomination." Prayer is the easy part; keeping the hindrances out of the way is what takes the effort.

CHAPTER TWELVE

WHOM DOES
GOD HEAR?

There is a parable in Luke 18 about a Pharisee and a tax collector who both went to the temple to pray. The Pharisee spends all his time reminding God how good he is. He tells God that he is obviously more righteous than the tax collector. With a boastful, self-righteous attitude he reminds God of all the things he does for Him. At the same time, the tax collector is around the corner in the temple and cannot even bring himself to raise his eyes to heaven, but beats his chest and asks God to have mercy on him, because he is an unworthy sinner. Jesus tells us that the tax collector went home justified and the Pharisee did not. Jesus sums it up by saying, "For everyone who exalts himself will be humbled, and he who humbles himself will be exalted." God wants us to recognize and confess our sins without justifying ourselves with comparisons to other sinners. Jesus also corrects the mistaken notion that righteousness is our doing, when in reality it is the product of the grace of God. Attitude is so important. We must remain humble and never allow pride to enter in.

God's Word declares in Psalm 34:15-17, "The eyes of the Lord are on the righteous, and His ears are open to their cry. The face of the Lord is against those who do evil, to cut off the remembrance of them from the earth. The righteous cry out, and the Lord hears and delivers them out of all their troubles." When we give our hearts to Jesus, we become righteous because of His work at the cross.

God also hears the prayers of those who fear Him. This use of the word *fear* means love and respect. In Psalm 34, He tells us there is "no want for those who *fear* Him and those who seek the Lord shall not lack any good thing." Psalm 145:18 says, "The Lord is near to all who call upon Him in truth. He will fulfill the desire of those who *fear* Him; He also will hear their cry and save them."

Several years ago, Sandra was living in a small one-bedroom apartment situated right on a busy street. It was so noisy, and the fumes from the street were so bad that she could not open her patio doors or windows. She could not afford to move, and because she was new in town, she did not know anyone who could have helped her. She found herself feeling frustrated and complaining about her bad situation. One day God impressed upon her heart to stop complaining and just ask Him for a bigger place. Now understand that, financially and logistically, moving into a bigger apartment was just not possible in the natural. But we are learning that nothing is impossible with our God.

Once Sandra prayed and asked Him, she began to believe it. Even though she could not see how it could be done, she just started thanking Him for her new, bigger and better apartment. She thanked Him for the small one He had already provided, and thanked Him for the new one that was coming. A few months later, there was a terrible rainstorm and the rain came down between Sandra's bedroom wall and the outside wall. As a result, she could no longer live in this apartment. The landlady felt so bad because Sandra had only been there a short time, and offered her a larger two bedroom apartment farther off the street for the same rent. The landlady even transferred the deposit and did not deduct any fees for cleaning.

Because the two apartments were in the same complex, it was simple for Sandra to make several trips after work each night. She simply took things out of her smaller apartment and moved them over to her new apartment, which left only the large items that she was unable to move on her own. God had that worked out as well. Sandra had just begun working in the office of a warehouse business, and when she told her coworkers that she was moving, the manager and two drivers not only offered to help her, they gave her the use of the company truck as well. Moving day was simple. The big guys arrived and moved all the heavy stuff right into her new apartment. God took care of every detail and all Sandra had to do was ask, believe Him, stay out of it, and let Him do it. Psalm 32:10 (Amplified) says, "Many are the sorrows of the wicked, but he who trusts in, relies on, and confidently leans on the Lord shall be compassed about with mercy and with loving kindness."

We mere humans cannot possibly see the big picture the way God does. That is why He tells us to trust Him; it is our job to believe that His Word is true and *alive*. When we try to work things out on our own, we are saying that we do not trust God to work things out on our behalf. The Word says in Romans 1:17, "The just shall live by faith." If we are to be justified, we must learn to live by faith.

CHAPTER THIRTEEN

DID I SAY THAT?

A group of frogs were traveling through the woods when two of them fell into a deep pit. All the other frogs gathered around the ditch. When they saw how deep it was, they told the two frogs there was no chance for survival. The two frogs ignored the comments and tried to jump out of the pit with all their might. The other frogs kept telling them to stop—they were as good as dead. Finally, one of the frogs listened to what they were saying and gave up. He fell down and died. The other frog continued to jump as high as he could. Finally, with the crowd of frogs still yelling at him to quit, he jumped even higher and made it out. When he got out, the other frogs said, "Did you not hear us?" The frog explained to them that he was deaf and he thought they were encouraging him and cheering him on the entire time! This story has a powerful lesson according to Proverbs 18:21. Our tongues contain the power of life and death. An encouraging word to someone who is down can lift them up and help them make it through the day, while a destructive word to someone who is down can be all it takes to kill their spirit.

We pray with people all the time who have not fulfilled their potential because of words spoken over them when they were young.

- "You will never amount to anything."
- "You are stupid."
- "No one will ever love you."
- "You are fat, you are ugly, and you are unwanted."
- "You were a mistake."

We need to realize that all of these statements are contrary to what God says and thinks about us. Considering that He handcrafted each and every one of us in His own image, we need to learn to listen to what *He* says about us rather than what the world has to say.

Encouraging words have the opposite effect as in the frog story. The deaf frog thought they were telling him that he could do it, so he reached beyond himself and did. When Louise's son Ken was about thirty years old, he told her about a contest his union was having. She asked him if he was going to enter, and he told her no, that he did not stand a chance.

Louise encouraged him to try it, not realizing that her words of encouragement still carried any weight with her grown son. A few weeks later, he mentioned in passing that he had entered the contest but had not won. Louise was very proud of him for trying and told him so. That day she learned a very valuable lesson as a parent. She realized that she still had influence over him even though he was an adult.

On another occasion, Louise's daughter Pam, a married mother of a toddler, she decided she wanted to go to nursing school. In her younger years, she had been an average student who never liked school, so this was a stretch. At the time, having no idea how difficult it would be to become an RN, Louise kept telling her that she could do it. At one point, Pam was attending three different college campuses in order to cover all the required classes. She believed God every step of the way and so did Louise. Each time she would have a test, the two women would pray and ask the Holy Spirit to make up the difference between what Pam knew and what she needed to know. Pam did her part by studying and trusting, and God did His part by making her an honor student. Louise did her part by encouraging her every day, even though there were days she was just not sure Pam had what it would take to get her degree. Many years have passed since Pam graduated and she is now a fine, caring, Christian nurse. These two examples show us just how much influence and responsibility we have as parents.

Not only do we need to encourage others, we need to encourage ourselves as well. Many times we say negative things to and about ourselves.

- "I am fat."
- "I cannot do that. I am stupid. I am too old. My nose is too big."
- "No one wants me. I will never find a husband or a wife."
- "I'll never have anything. My money comes in one hand and goes out the other."

Proverbs 6:2 says, "You are *snared* by the words of your mouth. You are *taken* by the words of your mouth." God says it twice in the same verse; our words will make us or break us. We create our own reality by the words we speak and the words we listen to. The Word of God should be the only word we listen to. Our Bible tells us who we are, what we are capable of, and what we are entitled to as children of God, but how many of us actually *believe* what God says about us?

We must stop listening to the world and believe what God says about us so we can become what God created us to be. We must stop beating ourselves up over the past so much that we are not productive in the present. We need to say, "That was then and this is now." Remember, when we received Christ into our hearts, we became new creations in Him. All that old garbage was washed away; we must now line up our mouth with what God says about us.

Some Christians struggle with feeling powerless or guilty over their circumstances, but Jesus tells us in Mark 11:23-24, "...for assuredly I say to you, whoever says to this mountain be removed and cast into the sea and does not doubt in his heart, but believes that these things that he says will be done, he will have whatever he *says*. Therefore I say to you, whatever things you ask, when you pray, *believe* that you *receive* them and you will have them."

We need to stand on promises just like this one when we pray. We need to pray God's Word back to Him, reminding Him of His promises. We can pray things like, "Thank you, Father, that goodness and mercy follow me all the days of my life" (Psalm 23:6), and, "Lord, bless me today and help me to be a blessing" (1 Chronicles 4:10). By praying what God has promised, we are calling blessings into our lives that are based solely on His Word, and when we pray these things, we must expect them to come to pass. Even those who are not experiencing it now will see it manifest when they begin to declare it, and those who are already experiencing goodness and mercy in their lives need to continue to declare it to keep it coming.

When you ask Louise's husband, Pete, how he is doing, he will answer you, "I am blessed going in and coming out." People think that this is just a fancy way to say he is fine, but in reality, he is declaring blessings over his life every time he quotes Deuteronomy 28:6. And because of his constant declaration, he lives a blessed life.

God's Word says we walk in His favor, and we believe it is true. We say that we walk in the "FOG" (Favor Of God). People laugh, but we have said it over and over and it has consistently manifested in our lives. We are always looking for the FOG; everywhere and every day and we are quick to thank our Father in heaven for His favor.

God says in Jeremiah 33:3, "Call unto me and I will answer you and show you great and mighty things that you know not of." So many times over the years we have confessed this scripture in prayer with people and watched God perform His Word right before our eyes. For anyone with their back against a wall, this is the first scripture that should be prayed. It is sometimes a tough one to believe, but we suggest praying it until it is manifest. We cannot emphasize enough the importance of praying God's promises back to Him. Deuteronomy 4:11 says, "God is not a man that He should lie." This tells us that everything He says in scripture must be true, and if He says to call on His name and He will show us great and mighty things, then that is exactly what He will do.

Another scripture to have memorized is Deuteronomy 31:6, which says, "Be strong and of good courage, fear not, nor be afraid of them, for the Lord thy God, it is He that goes with thee: He will not fail thee." Instead of brooding about negative circumstances, we must learn to speak His Word over them. When we say things that are contrary to His Word, God cannot do anything. He can only do what He said in His Word. That is why it is so important that we continually speak His Word over our circumstances: over our marriages, over our children, over our finances. When we speak His Word, we bring life into the situation, but when we speak our own negative words, we bring death into the situation.

Let us be clear on this. We are not preaching "the power of positive thinking" or "name it and claim it." Instead, it is what we call "God thinking" and "God speaking," and it is not easy. It requires obedience, faith, trust, gratefulness and praise. Some people will look at this and say we are in denial, but we would say we are in obedience to God's Word, which tells us to "call things that be not as though they were," until they become. God has the answer for every situation. All we have to do is look it up in His Word, the Bible. It is our instruction book. God gave us these scriptures so we would know who we are; so we would know what we can do and what we can have. The Bible says that God "watches over His Word to perform it." When we say His Words, He confirms them. He said, "Put me in remembrance of my Word."

We are not saying that if we are sick and someone asks us how we are, we should lie. It is a matter of attitude. We simply say, "I am a healing in progress. The Word says I am healed and I am standing on the Word." That is a far cry from dwelling on our illness and making people sorry they ever asked!

Speaking God's Word can be applied to any problem we might have. For those who are unemployed and are asked if they have found a job yet, we recommend saying something to the effect of, "Not yet. God is still preparing the perfect job for me—a job that pays well and that I will love." God promised in Deuteronomy 16 that He would bless the work of our hands; it is our job to find the promise, stand on it, and declare it.

CHAPTER FOURTEEN

WHEN YOUR HEART FEELS BROKEN

The perfect world God created in the first chapters of Genesis no longer exists. From the moment Adam and Eve disobeyed God and ate from the Tree of Knowledge, our world has been subject to death and decay, and every one of us has had to deal with the grief that comes with loss. Some have lost parents, spouses or children to either death or divorce. Some have had meaningful relationships dissolve through no fault of their own. Others have lost their health, their jobs, or even their pets.

Loss and grief are members of the same family and there are as many ways to express grief as there are reasons for being grieved. Some people internalize their grief and withdraw from other people. Some might stay in bed and not answer the doorbell or the phone. Others externalize their grief, sometimes in the form of rebellion. We often see this in children when their parents get a divorce or they lose a parent through death. They become rebellious, disobedient, or self-destructive.

Anger is a common by-product of loss, and often instead of directing anger at the loss, we blame God. Feeling helpless or out of control in the situation, we ask God, "Why did you let this happen to me?" or "Why are you doing this to me?" The enemy takes great pleasure in this, but we have a loving God, who understands that His children would have all these emotions and made provision to deal with them.

Psalm 34:18 tells us, "The Lord is near to those who have a broken heart." In Psalm 147:3, we see that "He heals the brokenhearted and binds up their wounds (curing their pains and their sorrows)" (Amplified).

Louise knows her God heals broken hearts, because she watched Him do it in her own family. When her daughter Pam was in her teens, her best friend was an older guy named Russ. Russ always wanted the relationship to be more, but the six-year age difference was too great, and they went their separate ways. Every now and then, they would run into each other, and as the years passed, the six years between them no longer seemed to be such a big gap.

Russ and Pam realized that they had loved each other all along, and they began dating. They were inseparable and finally got married. Four years into a wonderfully happy marriage, Russ was diagnosed with cancer. With Pam by his side and much prayer, he fought the cancer for three years. Sadly, Russ passed away, not because of the cancer, but because of a medical error. Pam was devastated.

To make matters worse, Pam's boss insisted that she come back to work within a week of his death. She gathered up all that she had within her and went to work, but she called Louise every day because she was so brokenhearted. Louise would quote God's Word to her and tell her to give her pain and grief to Jesus because He was the only one who could bear this awful burden.

Pam had the wisdom in the midst of her grief to tell God, "I do not know what to do. I need you to be my husband and take care of me. Holy Spirit, please come and fill me and heal my broken heart." By asking God for help, she was able to let go of her anger at the situation. It was very difficult to stay mad at God while praying for his aid.

Pam was a registered nurse at a veterans home, and she would walk the halls inviting the Holy Spirit to come into her heart and comfort her. She would quietly sing to herself, "Come Holy Spirit, I need you." Of course she cried. Of course she was sad. At times she felt like her life was over. She saw no future for herself, but even in the midst of all those feelings, she was able to give her grief to Him, moment by moment. As the days and weeks went by, Louise could see the dark clouds in her daughter's eyes begin to clear.

After a few weeks, Pam's doctor suggested that she seek out grief counseling. She began to attend a grief counseling group and did everything they told her to do while still giving her grief to Jesus. At one point, she called Louise to say, "Mom, I am so much better off than these people. There is a lady there that lost her husband four years ago and is still a mess!"

Finding her strength in Christ, Pam was moving toward wholeness. She told Louise that God was teaching her to look at things from His perspective. Instead of seeing what she had lost, she was beginning to see those seven years with Russ as a precious gift from God. When she received that revelation, she could finally think about Russ every day, several times a day, without a desperate longing and ache in her heart. God did what He promised in His Word, and Jesus came to heal her broken heart!

In less than a year, Louise had the privilege of watching her daughter not only find healing, but joy as well, and Pam has come to a place where she can use her tragic experience and what she learned from it to minister to others who feel brokenhearted.

We can follow Pam's example in the midst of our own losses. We must always lean on the promises of God and be so thankful that He has provided His promises for just such times. In the Sermon on the Mount in Matthew 5:4, Jesus tells us that we can expect to have comfort in our mourning and we will be blessed. We like how the Amplified Bible states this scripture. "Blessed *and* enviably happy (with a happiness produced by the experience of God's favor and especially conditioned by the revelation of His matchless grace) are those who mourn for they shall be comforted."

Comfort comes when we remember God will take our mourning and turn it into something He can be glorified in. He will be blessed, and we will be blessed. We find that assurance in Isaiah 61:2-3, in which God promises "...to comfort all who mourn, to console those who mourn in Zion, to give them *beauty for ashes*, the *oil of joy* for mourning, the *garment of praise* for the spirit of heaviness: that they may be called trees of righteousness, the planting of the Lord, that *He may be glorified*" (NKJ).

It is also important to remember that God loves us and will not forsake us. Psalm 56 tells us our tears are so precious to God that He keeps every one in a bottle; not one tear has fallen from our eye that has escaped his loving and watchful gaze. God is with us, no matter how deeply we are hurting. He is right beside us all the time, and if we are willing to *trust* Him with our hurts, He will heal our broken hearts.

CHAPTER FIFTEEN

PRAISE AND GRATITUDE

Hebrews 13:14-15 says, "...for here we have no permanent city, but we are looking for the one which is to come, through Him, therefore, let us constantly *and* at all times offer up to God a sacrifice of praise, which is the fruit of lips that thankfully acknowledge *and* confess *and* glorify His name" (Amplified). This scripture exhorts us to offer praise to God *constantly*, which means we should do so whether or not we feel like it, and regardless of the circumstances. That is why it is referred to as a sacrifice.

In our years in ministry, we have learned that praise is a powerful force. It keeps the enemy at bay. As we praise God, we hear the words coming from our mouth and we are encouraged, and in the spirit realm, it causes demons to flee. In every situation, we can always find something for which to praise God, even if it as simple as praising Him for always being right by our side. We believe that we can praise our way out of any mess we find ourselves in. Scripture tells us that God inhabits the praises of His people, and we know that darkness and light cannot exist in the same place. In the Old Testament, praise was so important to God that He commanded a "Praise Company" to lead all the armies into battle. The first line in the defense consisted of those whose job it was to praise God.

It is important to remember that we do not praise God to move Him, but rather as we praise Him, we increase our faith to receive the answer He has already provided. All we really need to do is remind ourselves of who He is. The very definition of praise is the act of acclaiming, honoring, and exalting. It is an expression of approval or admiration. It is also the worship and reverence accorded a deity. It is ardent devotion. In other words, praise is what we say *about* God, and worship is how we do it.

Praise is not enough. In addition, we must never, not even for a moment, forget to be grateful to our God for His mercy and grace. First Thessalonians 5:18 says, "Thank (God) in everything (no matter what the circumstances may be, be thankful and give thanks), for this is the will of God for you (who are) in Christ Jesus (the Revealer and Mediator of that will)" (Amplified).

The closer we draw to God, the more we will develop a grateful heart. This closeness produces a love for Him that opens our eyes in a way that we begin to see Him at work in everything. By having a grateful heart, even if we are unemployed, we can be grateful to God, because He knows exactly where we are and is working behind the scenes to bring us a job. Even if it is not the job we thought we wanted, we must be grateful that He is ordering our steps and He has put us where we are for reasons we may never know. We cannot allow ourselves to grumble. Instead, we must be grateful and look for ways to honor Him and bless others. This is only one small example, but the principle works in every situation.

CHAPTER SIXTEEN

THE LOVE CHAPTER

Matthew 22:37-40 commands, "You shall love the Lord your God, with all your soul, and with all your mind." This is the first and greatest commandment Jesus gives us, and it coincides with the first four of the Ten Commandments of the Old Testament. The second command that Jesus gives us is to love our neighbors as ourselves, which sums up the last six of the Ten Commandments. Jesus goes on to tell us that on these two commandments hang all the law and the prophets. As we said earlier, spiritual laws govern all life. All these laws hang on the master law of love, because God is love. God is also life, and without Him there is no life. God is very clear here that He wants us to love Him and others. You see, if we love others in the way He instructs us, we will not steal from them, we will not covet what they have, we will not lie to them or about them, and we will not commit adultery. Jesus summed up all ten of the original commandments in his two commandments of love.

The Bible tells us in Galatians 5:6 that faith works by love, and then devotes an entire chapter of 1 Corinthians to telling us what love is and what love is not. In "The Love Chapter," 1 Corinthians13:8 tells us love never fails, and verse 13 sums it all up with God instructing us to live by faith, hope and love—with love being the greatest of these.

There was a time in Sandra's life when she stood on these verses regarding her relationship with her children. At the time, things were tough and she did not have the relationship with them that she desired. Time and time again, she would remind herself that love never fails. No matter what they did or what they said, she would love them and continue to tell them so. It took some time, but they began to realize their mother really did love them, and now they all enjoy a wonderful relationship. Sandra knows without a doubt it is because love never fails.

As we mentioned earlier, love is so important to God because He is love. If we are to be His "little anointed ones," then we must find ways to be ambassadors of His love. There are many ways to walk in love. Love is getting up in the middle of the night to help a friend without grumbling. Love is refusing to participate in gossip. Love is looking for the best in someone rather than focusing on their shortcomings. Love is looking for ways to bless others—not just those in need, but anyone who could use an unexpected blessing. Love is keeping our mouths shut when anger rises up in us. Love is asking for forgiveness even though we are sure we are right. Love is putting the needs of others before our own and doing what is right, even when we do not want to.

Walking in love is not always easy, but because it is so important to God, we must make it a priority. We must make the decision daily to walk in love, and pray daily that the Holy Spirit will help. As we plant seeds of love, we will begin to reap a harvest of love. We like that about God. He is full of rewards. If we are to be like God, who loves us so much just the way we are, then we must love others just the way they are.

It is important to remember that contrary to popular belief, love is a decision and not a feeling. In fact, all of our emotions are controlled by the decisions we make. Emotions can be very valuable to us and to God, but only if we choose to use them correctly and not abuse them. It is what we decide to do with these emotions that is important. James 5:16 tells us, "Confess your trespasses to one another, and pray for one another that you may be healed. *The effective fervent prayer of a righteous man avails much*" (NKJ). We like the way the Amplified version says it: "*The earnest (heartfelt, continued) prayer of a righteous man makes tremendous power available (dynamic in its working)."* This is an example of putting an emotion to work in a positive way.

On the other hand, dwelling on a negative emotion can have a significant impact on our health and general well being. Proverbs 12:25 says, "…anxiety in the heart of a man causes depression…" and Proverbs 17:22 tells us, "a merry heart does good like medicine, but a broken spirit dries the bones."

Emotions should never be ignored or accepted blindly. In John 12:27, Jesus tells His Father in heaven that His soul is deeply troubled, even though He knows this is His purpose for coming. In the end, He makes the decision not to dwell on the negative when He says in verse 28, "Father, glorify your name."

While on earth, Jesus was a human and as such, had all the same emotions that we have. The major difference between us is that He *never sinned* because of His emotions. He suffered loneliness (Mark 15:34), frustration (Mark 8:12), and anger (Matthew 21:12-13). He experienced sorrow (Matthew 23:37), wept (John 11:35 and Luke 19:41), and rejoiced (Luke 10:21). There is no emotion we can experience that Jesus did not also experience during His human life, and we can take comfort in this fact as we deal with our human emotions on a day-to-day basis.

CHAPTER SEVENTEEN

OUR HEALING IS SEALED

Scripture tells us in Hebrews 10:23, "So let us seize and hold fast and retain without wavering the hope we cherish and confess, and our acknowledgement of it, for He who promised is reliable (sure) and faithful to His word" (Amplified).

We keep coming back to the promises of God and the fact that we can believe His Word is truth. In both the old covenant (Mosaic Law) and our new covenant (salvation through Christ), healing is one of our provisions. God heals the sinner because of His mercy. He heals the believer because of His covenant. As children of the covenant, our healing is sealed.

It is important to believe God *before* we get sick. It is better to believe God to walk in divine health (which is His best) than to have to believe

Him for healing. That is why we have to be rooted and grounded in the Word. Proverbs 4:20-24 (NKJ) says, "My son, give attention to my word; incline your ear to my sayings. Do not let them depart from your eyes; keep them in the midst of your heart; for they are life to those who find them, and health to all their flesh." Living in divine health means that we must be aware that we already have the healed body promised by God. When we do experience symptoms of illness, we need to realize it is the enemy of our soul trying to destroy our body. Therefore, the godly, faith-filled response is to become aggressive about our healing. First Peter 2:24 tells us we are healed by Christ's stripes. In His death and resurrection, we have life and health. For this reason, we believe that a good place to start the warfare for our health is to take communion. We do not need to be in a church to receive communion. In fact, we keep the communion elements on hand for just such occasions. When we take communion, we do so in remembrance of what Jesus did for us at Calvary—the precious blood He spilled for our salvation, the beatings He endured for our healing, and the new covenant promises.

Jesus has already paid the price for our healing, so when we are facing an attack of Satan, we need to focus on Jesus all day and all night. As we keep our minds focused on Jesus and our healing, we push the thoughts of our sickness away. All during the day, we should be thanking God for our healing. We like to put on some praise music or tapes of scripture readings. Whatever we choose, the idea is to fill our minds with the Word of God. As we remind ourselves of God's healing provision, our faith will reach out and receive our healing. Remember, "Faith comes by hearing the Word of God" (Romans 10:17). We must get serious about hearing the Word. When Satan launches a serious attack against us, we cannot mess around. We must be on the offensive for *every* attack against us that comes our way.

Several years back, Sandra went to see her doctor because she was having dizzy spells. The doctor sent her to a neurologist, who recommended she have an MRI. The results revealed a kidney-shaped tumor in the lower part of her brain, and because this tumor was so close to the nerves controlling the right side of the face, the doctor was reluctant to go in to remove it for fear it could damage her ability to swallow and smile.

The night of her diagnosis, Sandra was pondering all the information and trying to figure out just what exactly it meant to her. In the midst of all of her thoughts, God brought a word to her mind: *trespasser*. She realized that this word applied to this tumor, as it was a trespasser and had no right to be present in her body. She immediately began to pray and ask God to remove it. Sandra found healing scriptures to meditate on and made sure, from that point on, to speak only words of faith about the situation. She even decided not to claim the tumor, and never once referred to it as "*her* tumor." As far as she was concerned, and according to the word

God had given her, it was a trespasser. Louise stood in agreement with her for the tumor to disappear.

Every day Sandra stood on the promises of God and reminded herself of His power and faithfulness. She took communion with diligence. Several times a day, she would command the tumor to leave her body in the name of Jesus Christ. Most importantly, she *believed* God. Isaiah 26:3 says, "You will guard him and keep him in perfect *and* constant peace whose mind (both its inclination and its character) is stayed on You, because he commits himself to you, leans on you *and* hopes confidently in you" (Amplified). God is telling us here that if we keep our attention on Him and His Word, our minds will be free from doubt and unbelief. If we trust His Word, we trust Him.

Three months after the initial diagnosis, another MRI revealed that the tumor was slightly smaller. Sandra rejoiced, because she could actually see God at work. But even if she had not seen God at work, it was still her job to keep believing, keep praying, and keep commanding the tumor to leave her body. As long as we have breath, we have to believe. That is what faith is all about. Six months later, Sandra had another MRI, followed by yet another six months after that. The final MRI showed that the tumor was no longer in her brain, and a conversation with the doctor confirmed the test results. The "trespasser" had left her body. Praise God!

James 5:15 tells us, "The prayer of faith shall save the sick, and the Lord shall raise him up; and if he has committed sins, they shall be forgiven him" (KJV). This is a New Testament scripture. Some people believe healings are not for today. They believe only Jesus had the power to heal. In truth, Mark 16:17-18 (KJV) answers this quite clearly: "And these signs shall follow them that believe; in my name shall they cast out devils; they shall speak with new tongues; they shall take up serpents; and if they drink any deadly thing, it shall not hurt them; they shall lay hands on the sick and they shall recover." Does this verse tell us to test God by drinking poison and holding deadly animals? Absolutely not! Jesus is simply charging us to have the faith to use His name to do the things He did, and then promising us that signs and wonders will follow.

God tells us His ways are higher than our ways, so it makes sense that we would want to use His ways. We are not saying we should not do what the doctor says, or throw out the prescribed medications to treat the illness. It is possible to do everything in the natural to be healed and still operate in the supernatural by believing God and His promises.

When we are given a negative report from the doctor, we have a choice. We can accept the negative diagnosis and the consequences it brings, or we can choose to believe in a supernatural God. We have nothing to lose. When we make the choice to believe God and operate in the supernatural realm, every-thing in our flesh will scream out a list of "what if's," but we must be ready to do battle with the enemy and hold our holy ground. Above all else, we must not lose faith in the Word of God.

HEALING SCRIPTURES (NKJ)

Prov.4:20-23 says, "My son, give attention to my words; Incline your ear to my sayings. Do not let them depart from your eyes; Keep them in the midst of your heart; For they are life to those who find them and health to all their flesh. Keep your heart with all diligence. For out of it spring the issues of life." In other words, "My words are medicine to all your body."

The following are some of the scriptures you can take like medicine every day. There are so many and we encourage you to dig into God's Word and find more.

So Abraham prayed to God; and God healed Abimelech, his wife, and his female servants. Then they bore children. (Gen. 20.17)

If you diligently heed the voice of the Lord your God and do what is right in His sight, give ear to His commandments and keep all His statutes, I will put none (or permit none) of the diseases on you which I have brought on the Egyptians. For I am the Lord who heals you. (Ex. 15:26)

You shall walk in all the ways which the Lord your God has commanded you, that you may live and that it may be well with you, and that you may prolong your days in the land which you shall possess. (Deut. 5:33)

And the Lord will take away from you all sickness, and will afflict you with none of the terrible diseases of Egypt which you have known..... (Deut. 7:15)

Thus says the Lord, the God of David your father; "I have heard your prayer, I have seen your tears; surely I will heal you." (2 Kings 20:5)

For the eyes of the Lord run to and fro throughout the whole earth to show Himself strong on behalf of those whose heart is loyal to Him. (2 Chr. 16:9)

Lord my God, I cried out to You, And You healed me. (Ps. 30:20)

Many are the afflictions of the righteous, But the Lord delivers him out of them all. (Ps. 34:19)

The Lord will strengthen him on his bed of illness; You will sustain him on his sickbed. (Ps. 41:3)

No evil shall befall you, Nor shall any plague come near your dwelling; For He shall give His angels charge over you, To keep you in all your ways. In their hands they shall bear you up, Lest you dash your foot against a stone. You shall tread upon the lion and the cobra, The young lion and the serpent you shall trample underfoot. Because he has set his love upon Me, therefore I will deliver him; I will set him on high, because he has known My name. He shall call upon Me, and I

116

will answer him; I will be with him in trouble; I will deliver him and honor him. With long life I will satisfy him, and show him My salvation. (Ps. 91:10-16)

Who forgives all your iniquities, Who heals all your diseases. (Ps. 103:3)

He heals the brokenhearted and binds up their wounds. (Ps. 147:3)

Fear not, for I am with you; Be not dismayed, for I am your God. I will strengthen you, Yes I will help you; I will uphold you with My righteous right hand. (Is. 41:10)

Surely He has borne our griefs and carried our sorrows; Yet we esteemed Him stricken, Smitten by God, and afflicted. But He was wounded for our transgressions; The chastisement for our peace was upon Him. And by His stripes we are healed. (Is. 53:4-5)

"For I will restore health to you and heal you of your wounds," says the Lord. (Jer. 30:17)

Behold, I will bring it health and healing; I will heal them and reveal to them the abundance of peace and truth. (Jer. 33:6)

And behold, a leper came and worshiped Him saying, "Lord, if You are willing, You can make me clean." Then Jesus put out His hand and touched him, saying, "I am willing, be cleansed." Immediately his leprosy was cleansed. (Matt. 8:2-3)

But when Jesus knew it, He withdrew from there, and great multitudes followed Him, and He healed them all. (Matt. 12:15)

And when Jesus went out He saw a great multitude; and He was moved with compassion for them, and healed their sick. (Matt. 14:14)

All through the Bible, God tells us that His will for His children is to be whole and healthy. He sent His son Jesus to purchase that wholeness. These are but a few examples of God's will for us. Meditate on these day and night until they dwell deeply in your heart and search for more and you will walk in health and wholeness.

CHAPTER EIGHTEEN

A New Meaning for The Name Savior

Louise recently had a profound opportunity to put into practice much of what we have shared in this book. In the fall of 2005, Louise's daughter Pam decided to take Louise to Mexico for her birthday. They arrived in Cancun late on a Saturday night and checked into a five-star hotel. When they awoke the next morning, they found themselves on the most beautiful beach they had ever seen. The water was crystal clear and turquoise blue, and the weather was fantastic.

Over the next few days, Louise and Pam thoroughly enjoyed their vacation. They spent time on the beach—Pam in the sun, and Louise under a grass-like canopy called a *palapa*. They took several day trips to see the sights of Mexico and experienced incredible service from the hotel staff.

While they were in the water on Wednesday, they encountered a young girl who shared that she had received a phone call from her mother, wanting her to return home due to hurricane conditions heading their way. Alarmed by this news, they returned to their room, where Pam received a call from a friend in Canada confirming that record-breaking (category five) Hurricane Wilma was due to make landfall in Mexico sometime over the next couple of days.

Even though they were scheduled to fly home early the next morning, Pam immediately began making calls in order to move up their reservations so they could get out of Mexico right away. In the meantime, the Holy Spirit reminded Louise that the Bible says perfect peace comes to those whose minds are stayed on Christ (Isaiah 26:3). She was filled with such an overwhelming sense of peace that she went to have the massage she had scheduled earlier in the day. Pam continued to make calls and pack bags, and was a little irritated with Louise's seeming indifference to their situation. By the time Louise returned from her wonderful massage, Pam had discovered that there was no way to get out any earlier than their planned flight at 11:30 the next morning. With nothing else to do, they made their way down to dinner and made every attempt to enjoy, and even savor, the last night of their vacation together.

The next morning after breakfast, they packed up their belongings, made their way to the lobby, and checked out. Because Pam had already made arrangements for a courier service to pick them up and get them to the airport at a designated time, they were not concerned about their departure. Unfortunately, instead of being picked up by their service, they were informed that the hurricane was close enough to force the closure of the airport. In addition, while the hotel *was* evacuating hotel patrons, Louise and Pam had already checked out, so they were no longer the responsibility of the hotel. They were on their own.

Many of the people in the lobby were upset and frightened, and while Pam made attempts to reach the taxi service, Louise tried to encourage a new bride who was visibly shaken. Louise was able to calm the newlywed, but Pam was not getting anywhere with transportation issues. Hurricane Wilma's impending landfall was causing confusion and uncertainty, and the operator at the taxi service was no exception as he tried to figure out what to do. In the meantime, the Holy Spirit continued to minister to Louise's spirit, bringing comforting scriptures to her mind. Isaiah 40:31 assured her that if she waited on the Lord, she would rise up on wings as eagles. Hebrews 13:5 reminded her that God would never leave her or forsake her, and she continued to rest in perfect peace.

The crowd in the hotel lobby increased in size and anxiety. Some were able to leave on busses with the tour guides who were responsible for them, and it occurred to Louise and Pam that they had no one who would take care of them. No one, that is, except their Almighty God. Louise remembered Romans

8:31, which promised that if God was for her, no one could be against her. She quietly prayed that God would provide her and her daughter with everything they might need to weather this storm.

Several hours later—after much waiting and negotiating—Pam was able to get the company to agree to send a driver to take her and Louise to a shelter. After what seemed like hours, a man finally showed up and led them to a van. He loaded their luggage, and as he got into the driver's seat, Pam said, "You are taking us to a shelter, right?" The driver answered that he was taking the women to the airport. When Pam told him it was closed and he should take them to a shelter, he got angry and ordered them to get out of the van. He threw open the van's back door, unloaded their luggage on to the curb, and got back in the van and drove off—leaving Louise and Pam standing on the sidewalk in a state of shock.

And so it began all over again. Pam got back on the phone and made several calls in an attempt to get hold of the company again. When she finally got through to a representative, she was assured that another driver would be on the way to take care of them. Sure enough, an hour later a different, more polite driver showed up and loaded them and their belongings into the van. He assured them he was indeed taking them to a shelter at a hotel in Playa Del Carmen.

By this time, Louise and Pam had heard that the people in Cancun were being evacuated to schools, the Civic Center, and any other large place they could be sheltered. Unfamiliar with the geography, they assumed that the shelter they were headed for was inland. Little did they know, as the driver dropped them off and instructed them where to check in, that they were just two blocks from the beach at an all-inclusive vacation hotel.

Upon checking in, Louise and Pam were shown to their room and instructed to go down to the restaurant to get something to eat and drink. Shortly after they had finished dinner, the hotel manager stood up and announced in several languages to the large group that a very large hurricane would be making landfall soon, but the hotel staff was experienced and prepared and there was no need for concern. While all the people had rooms of their own, they were informed that they would all be gathered into one building to make it easier to distribute food and water. Everyone was assigned to a room with between six and fifteen other people and advised to take only personal items with them. They were told to pack all luggage in the closet of their individual rooms and to report to the group rooms by 8:00 p.m. Louise and Pam did as they were told and found themselves knocking on the door to room 102 at 6:00 p.m.

Phil and Abbie, a nice couple on holiday from England, answered the door to what, until this time, had been their personal hotel accommodations. They welcomed Louise and Pam into a small two-room suite with a king-sized bed in one room and a day bed and desk in the other. After a few minutes of small talk, Pam and Louise decided to go back to their room for pillows and sodas from the mini bar. By the time they returned, three other American women had arrived, followed by several more people, until the room was crowded with fifteen people.

One of the American women, who had a domineering personality, immediately took charge of assigning space. She could tell that Pam was frightened, and suggested that Louise and Pam take the day bed. Several other people had already claimed the bed, leaving poor Phil and Abbie with nowhere to sleep. About this time, one of the ladies began to make jokes about God and the rapture and the weather, and while the jokes were offensive to Louise, she held her tongue. She knew she did not want to make any enemies in these close quarters, but she would certainly speak up if she needed to. Thankfully, the jokes subsided and everyone settled in.

The door to Room 102 closed at 10:00 p.m. Within hours the wind and rain started up. It was loud and violent. Everyone in the little suite could hear windows breaking and things hitting the outside of the cement building. Hotel staff delivered two sandwiches and water to everyone. Louise and Pam ate one each, putting the others away. They were not sure if or when more food would come, and this turned out to be a wise choice, as the next delivery would not be for twenty hours.

Sometime during Thursday night, water began to flood the room. Louise and Pam stayed dry on the daybed, but many on the floor were sleeping in water. Louise quietly thanked God that He had provided "high ground" for her and Pam. By this time, the electricity was out, with only two candles to light the room. But the bathroom was still working, and even though they had to wade through the water to reach it, they were all very glad to have it.

Even when the wind was blowing so hard that people had to literally hold the door shut, and even when the water flooding the room continued to rise, Louise never felt hopeless or terrified. She stood on the promises that God was continuously bringing to her mind, and she was able to experience perfect peace all throughout Friday and into Saturday. Late in the afternoon on Saturday the storm began to let up, and they were able to open the door. Despite the fact that rain was still falling and the wind was still gusting, several people left and went back to their individual rooms, but Louise and Pam stayed where they had been told to stay until the storm had completely passed.

By Sunday morning it had calmed down enough for everyone to venture outside. Debris and downed trees were scattered everywhere, and many windows had been blown out. Louise and Pam paid a visit to their personal room and found it flooded with water, with broken windows and no power or water, so they went back to Room 102. Power and hot water had been restored. Remembering that it was originally Phil and Abbie's room, Louise asked if she and Pam could use the showers. Phil and Abbie graciously complied. Later the four of them began to chat, and the conversation quickly turned to God and the Bible. Phil admitted that he had never studied the Bible and did not really believe it to be true, but Abbie was interested in hearing more.

Louise and Pam took this opportunity to share with them God's plan of salvation, then asked them if they would like to pray and accept Jesus as their Savior. Phil very kindly and politely declined, and Abbie told them she was not comfortable praying in front of someone else, so Pam told her how she could pray when she was alone. After that, Louise and Pam let it go, believing God's Word that what they had shared that day would not return void, but they did not part ways with Phil and Abbie. The foursome had bonded over their three-day ordeal, and together they spent the next several days attempting to pick up the pieces.

The first obstacle was communication. Louise and Pam were supposed to have flown home on Thursday, and they had not been able to get through to anyone to let them know they were OK. They knew their loved ones would be very concerned, so Phil was using his cell phone to try and get through. He finally reached Pam's daughter and let her know that they were both fine.

Meanwhile, a young American reporter who was staying in the hotel offered to take Louise and Pam to the mayor's office the next day to use the phone line. Desperate for information, the women agreed to meet her at 8:00 am. They had seen the devastation just outside the hotel compound, so it was not hard to believe reports that the airport in Cancun had been completely destroyed. They did not know what to do. When they finally reached the American Embassy in Cancun, they were advised that since they were being taken care of, it was a good idea to stay where they were. That reminded Louise that God had once told her that if she was unsure of what to do, she should do nothing and instead wait. This was confirmation in her spirit that they were in God's hands.

The next day, the American reporter and some of her friends decided to take a bus to another town five hours away to try and catch a flight to Mexico City. This sounded so tempting, but the Holy Spirit once again brought Isaiah 40:31 to Louise's mind and she chose to wait on the Lord and trust Him for His perfect timing. The Holy Spirit was so faithful through the entire ordeal, giving Louise just the right words at just the right times.

Little by little the hotel began to empty out. Tour groups were told by the embassies of their various countries to be ready to be picked up and bussed out, but Louise and Pam seemed stuck. Even Phil and Abbie had received instructions to get home. It was bittersweet to say goodbye to these new and dear friends. Louise and Pam were so happy that Phil and Abbie were going home, but sad to be separated from friends they had become so close to. While Phil was at the front desk, Louise had an opportunity to speak with Abbie. When Louise asked if she could pray with her, Abbie smiled and nodded. Louise prayed for blessings and safe travel, thanked God for the blessings Abbie and Phil had been to her, and then prayed that the Word of God she and Pam had planted would come alive and grow in Abbie. Saying goodbye was difficult, but Louise is certain she will see them again in heaven.

As it turned out, the news they had heard regarding the airport in Cancun was not true. It was not destroyed, but opened for business. Louise and Pam were unable to get through to them by phone, so Louise called her son and asked him if he could make arrangements to get them out on Saturday. He got back to them with confirmation, and finally, Louise and Pam had a flight out of Mexico—nine days after their original departure date.

At 8:30 a.m., Louise and Pam left the hotel for the airport. On the way they got a full picture of the devastation of Hurricane Wilma. They also got to see the local people out in force, cleaning up. There were no chainsaws to take care of fallen trees. Instead, the men were chopping wood with giant machetes. They were working very hard and fast to restore order to their beautiful country.

Upon their arrival at the airport, Louise and Pam had to find their way through hordes of people to the Aeromexico counter, where they were informed that they did not have a flight to Salt Lake City, only to Mexico City. The last thing the two women wanted was to go deeper into Mexico, so the man behind the counter suggested that they try Delta Airlines.

Hundreds of people stood between them and the Delta line, but they managed to make it. They both felt better just being at the airport, even if they did not yet have a flight out. At one point, someone came along counting passengers, because there was only one plane. Louise and Pam did not know if they had been included in the count, but Louise told Pam, "God can make a way where there is no way. He's the Way Maker, and I wouldn't be surprised if He sent us first class."

Three and a half hours later, they finally made it to the desk where they were greeted by a friendly man who entered their information in the computer. He told them that the destination of this plane was Atlanta, and Pam told him they did not care as long as they ended up in Montana. He shook his head as if he did not see how that would be possible, excused himself, and went to a supervisor. They spoke for a few minutes, then he returned to the computer, where he typed for what seemed like forever. Finally he told them that he could get them home if they were willing to spend the night in Salt Lake. They were so thankful, they did everything but jump over the counter and kiss him. He added that they would be flying into Atlanta FIRST CLASS! Once again, God was taking care of everything.

One more opportunity came for God to show His attention to detail to Louise and Pam. Before leaving the plane, they heard their names over the loudspeaker. When they found the ticket agent they had been instructed to see, he handed them vouchers for a motel room. He told them that when they exited the airport, they should look for the van. The only van they found was for an upscale, much more expensive hotel, but the driver told them that his hotel also honored these vouchers and that he could take them right away. A flight attendant told them they should take him up on it, so they did. They were blessed with a large suite with two big comfortable beds and a fireplace. By lunchtime the following day, they were back home, safe and sound, in Montana.

Hurricane Wilma was a horrific experience for many of the people who got caught in it. Some lost everything; others were injured or even killed. Louise and Pam saw this devastation first hand and came away from their experience changed. Louise was once again reminded that by obediently hiding God's Word in her heart, she was able to speak it, and in doing so, to experience perfect peace and wonderful blessings in the midst of chaos.

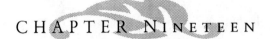

CHAPTER NINETEEN

GOD IS FAITHFUL!

We want to be very clear. We are not preaching things on the pages of this book that we ourselves have not experienced. We want simply to encourage others with the lessons we have learned in our own lives, so we can all walk on the high places God has provided for us.

We have watched God perform His Word over and over again for the past twenty-five years. We are not perfect people. We have fallen many times, but each time we have repented, gotten up, and found ourselves growing to a different level. God is faithful. He has met us where we were and taken us to higher places.

It is our desire for every person we come in contact with to be encouraged in our God and His faithfulness. If you will allow the Holy Spirit to do

His job, which is to lead you into all truth, you will receive the benefits of God's promises. Day by day, step-by-step, you will find yourself walking on high places.

Tapes and CD's Available from website
www.doubleportionministries.org

- GOD'S BLOOD COVENANT
- 6 PACK OF TEACHINGS (ASSORTED)
- HAPPY "NEW BIRTH" DAY
  (FOR NEW CHRISTIANS)
- YOUR TONGUE/BEST FRIEND, WORST ENEMY
- FREEDOM FROM WORRY
- FROM DARKNESS TO LIGHT TIMES TWO
  (OUR TESTIMONY)
- PRAYING WITH POWER
- COME ON, GET OUT OF THE BOAT
  (WALKING IN FAITH)
- WHAT'S IN YOUR CLOSET?
  (MATTERS OF THE HEART)
- HEALING SCRIPTURES

To order additional copies of

Walking On
High Places

Have your credit card ready and call:

1-877-421-READ (7323)

or please visit our web site at
www.pleasantword.com

Also available at:
www.amazon.com
and
www.barnesandnoble.com

Printed in the United States
71484LV00001B/172-210